A NEW

GUIDE TO IPSWICH,

CONTAINING NOTICES OF ITS

ANCIENT AND MODERN HISTORY,

ANTIQUITIES, BUILDINGS, INSTITUTIONS, SOCIAL AND
COMMERCIAL CONDITION.

BY J. WODDERSPOON.

IPSWICH:

J. M. BURTON.   LONDON: J. R. SMITH, SOHO.
MDCCCXLII.

TO THE

MAYOR AND CORPORATION

OF IPSWICH,

THIS SMALL VOLUME IS INSCRIBED BY

THE AUTHOR.

INDEX OF CONTENTS.

GUIDE TO IPSWICH.

—◦{}◦—

ORIGIN AND EARLY HISTORY OF IPSWICH, GRANT OF CHAR-
TERS, COMMERCE, ESTABLISHMENT OF MONASTERIES,
NOTICES OF CARDINAL WOLSEY, OF WOLSEY'S COLLEGE, &c.

IPSWICH, the most important town in the county
of Suffolk, is a thriving port, seated upon the river
Orwell, at its junction with the more humble stream
the Gipping. It is about fourteen miles distant
from the sea, though the Orwell is navigable for
vessels of considerable tonnage from its embro-
chure to the Wet Dock. The town contains twelve
churches and a chapel of ease connected with the
established church, eight dissenting places of worship, a Friends' meeting-house, one Roman Catholic
chapel, and a Jews' synagogue. The present number of inhabitants is about twenty-five thousand.

Like many towns whose origin is carried back
into the "dim antique," much doubt exists as to
the period when the first stones of the place received a name. Its original title might have been
very different to that which it now bears, though
its present cognomen can be traced through many

B

centuries, in ancient deeds, and the elder historica
documents, as Gyppesewich, Gyppeswic, Gippsewiz
Yppsewiche, Ippsewiche—Ipswich.

It is fair to be inferred, that the aborigina
Britons had a camp or town upon the site.   It i
certain that the Danes, in their incursions, foun(
some settlement of society upon the spot, as w<
have evidence, showing that previously to the yea1
1000 they paid the town a warlike visit, and threw
down the walls or fortifications which inclosed it.
Indeed there are several instances on record, in
which those great destroyers of the incipient foundations of civilization attacked the town of Ipswich.
As early as the year 882, a great contest took place
between this people and the British at the mouth
of the Orwell, when the Danes sustained a signal
defeat by the bravery of the celebrated Alfred.
Foiled for a while, the northern horde quitted the
neighbourhood, but in about eleven years afterwards
they made an attack upon the town, when they
reduced the enclosing ramparts to a heap of ashes.
Their inroad in the year 1000 has already been
stated, and in addition it must be recorded, that in
1012 and 1017 the Danes again made other assaults
upon the place, slaughtering all the inhabitants who
resisted their attacks, without mercy.

That part of the kingdom in which Ipswich is
situated, was very early formed into a portion of the
kingdom of the East Angles.   This monarchy was
bounded by the kingdom of Wessex on the south,
and Mercia on the West.   Its extent was eighty

miles in length by fifty-five in breadth, and included
the present counties of Norfolk and Suffolk, and a
portion of Cambridgeshire.   Its chief towns in
Suffolk existed upon the sites of Thetford, and it is
believed Ipswich.   The date of the erection of East
Anglia into a kingdom, is stated by the best historians at A. D. 575, and lasting 220 years, ceased in
existence as an independent province in 795.

The first king of East Anglia, of whom any mention has been made with certainty, is Uffa, a warlike
chieftain, who with twelve others landed in Britain
with a body of his countrymen, about A. D. 530.
He assumed the title of king of the East Angles
about forty-five years after his first landing, and
died, according to most authorities, in 581.   Being
the first monarch of his kingdom, his successors
added the names of Uffa, or Vffa, to their own,
thereby acknowledging the descent of the royal
dignity from him.   The next monarch was Titit,
the son of Uffa, whose reign and actions are involved in as much obscurity as those of his father.
Speed informs us that he reigned twenty years, but
Stow says only ten.   He died in the year 592, and
was succeeded in his possessions and dignity by
Redwald, the most active and illustrious monarch
of the entire heptarchy, over which he at last
became sole king.   The circumstances attending
the life of this latter prince, his conversion to
christianity, and the great regard paid by him to
the interests of that religion—were causes eminently
productive of the establishment of monasterial

institutions within this county. Although it is asserted, that the conversion of Redwald to the christian faith was not attended with permanently good effects, it being believed that he afterwards renounced its tenets and returned to paganism, yet there is sufficient on record to prove, that while he professed christianity, he performed its duties with conscientious exactness, and obliged his subjects to pay implicit attention to its precepts. There is little doubt that during his reign, some of those religious institutions in Suffolk, which were established almost immediately after the introduction of the new faith, owe their origin to his piety, and that largesses were conferred upon those individuals who devoted themselves to a monastic life and the study of christianity, as rewards for their good conduct. Erpwald, his son, who succeeded him, did not however receive the tenets of his faith from his father, but became indebted for a knowledge of christianity to Edwin, king of Northumberland, whom his father had succoured. Neither indeed did Edwin, who owed his conversion to Paulinus and his queen; but without doubt Redwald, by his mild demeanour, and peaceable conduct, except when roused to take vengeance on his enemies, set that good example to his subjects as, by softening the natural fierceness of their character, paved the way for the successful introduction of the true faith into his kingdom, as preached by its early followers. The conversion of Erpwald seems to have created a severe strife against him, and gave offence to a great number of his subjects. He was assassinated, professedly for his religion, by Richbert, a pagan warrior, who took upon himself the virtual sovereignty of East Anglia, although he did not assume the name of king. He contrived to govern for the space of three years, at the end of which period, Sigibert, or Sigchbert, who it is believed, on account of some jealousy on the part of his father against him, had retired into France, returned home, and mounted the throne. He was also a christian, having been converted from paganism while wandering abroad.

Sigibert, who became very ardent in the cause of the new religion he had professed, with the assistance of Felix and Furseus, made great progress in spreading its principles among his own subjects. Though brave, and possessing the becoming power of a sovereign over his people, he nevertheless wished to resign his government, and betake himself to the quiet of a monastery. To Sigbercht succeeded Annas, son of Enus and brother of Red-wald,* who came into power shortly after the death of the previous king. To Annas, succeeded Ethelred or Ethlhere. He was slain by Oswi, king of Northumberland. To him succeeded Aldulph, Alfwald, Beorne, Ethelred, and Ethelbert who was basely assassinated in 792, by his father-in-law Offa, king of Mercia. Upon his death the kingdom of East Anglia was again ravaged by the Mercians, with Offa at their head. A struggle of

* Nephew according to Brompton.

long duration followed, but in the end the East
Anglians were compelled to submit to the yoke of
their oppressors, until at length both powers in
their turn bowed their heads to the monarchy of
the West Saxons, under Egbert, in the early part of
the ninth century.   East Anglia, however, was
allowed to elect its own sovereign princes, the last
of which was Edmund, and was looked upon as a·
tributary province, retaining a portion of its former
independence through the favour of Egbert.

The monastery founded by Sigibert was intended
for the accommodation of a society of secular
monks, a community of men, not aware that by
attaching themselves to the comforts and morality
of a married life, they were missing, according to
the popish belief, the path leading to eternal happiness.   The question of celibacy or marriage was
contested with such spirit, and created so much
hostility in the land, that references to open combat
were almost made by the two parties to settle their
differences.   At length Dunstan, who from a monk
in the abbey of Glastonbury, raised himself by
furious zeal to the primacy, prevailed on the king,
Edgar to allow the ejection from the monasteries
throughout the kingdom, of "all those abominable
wretches that kept wives."   This charitable act
was permitted to be perpetrated, and in the course
of a few years the seculars being turned adrift, no
less than forty-eight monasteries were filled with
regular monks of the Benedictine order.   Great
numbers of the unfortunate beings thus deprived

of their homes perished with their families, in the high ways and bye ways of the land.* This event happened about the year 970.

Although there are not such authorities in existence as will lead us to the conclusion without doubt, that the origin of the town of Ipswich arose from an early settlement of a monastery upon its site, yet there is more than a reasonable probability for presuming it is to the establishment of a religious house upon the spot, that the incipient formation of the port and town is to be dated. Nearly all the towns of Suffolk that have attained any importance, date their origin from such sources. It is certain also, that in after times, when monachism ruled through the length and breadth of the land, Ipswich included within her walls many monasterial establishments, and that one of them, possessed an image of such pretended marvellous power and efficacy in the working of miracles, that when the yoke of the papal church was broken, this thing of wood was considered of sufficient importance to be taken from its sanctuary, carried up to London, and publicly destroyed. If we consider that the establishment of monasteries proved sufficiently attractive in almost all cases to induce the settlement of large bodies of laymen wherever they took root, we may form the opinion that the rule, and not the exception, prevailed as regards the town of the history of which we are now treating.

* Warner. Henry.

But from whatever cause the permanent establishment of Ipswich is to be attributed, it is certain that as early as 964 money was coined here, and specimens are extant of coins, struck at a mint possessed by the inhabitants, or perhaps the monks of Ipswich, from that period down to the times of Henry the third. Trade must therefore have made some efforts beyond mere barter, in the port, to render a medium of exchange at all necessary; and it is probable that when the Danes sacked the place, and razed the protecting walls that encompassed it, a portion of the early commerce of the time had been established within it to the benefit of the inhabitants, and the convenience of the surrounding neighbourhood.

Whatever might have been the condition of the town at a very ancient period, there are records extant shewing, that in the time of Richard the First, the inhabitants of Ipswich purchased their freedom of that monarch, and at the conclusion of his reign obtained a charter by similar means, from his successor John. The first great court of this incipient corporation was held openly, in the burial ground of St. Mary Tower church, and the bailiffs were elected from its body. Succeeding meetings of the corporation perfected its legal existence, even to the choice and adoption of a common seal.

This charter, granted by John, involved several conditions, and imposed burdens on the inhabitants, which may almost be considered as rendering free-

dom nugatory. The liberties of the town were to
be held from the monarch by the payment of an
annual sum, and "one hundred shillings more by
the hands of the provosts of Ipswich." The tolls
from the payment of which they were made exempt,
were only such as happened to be in existence at
the period of the grant, rendering the exemption of
but trifling moment; as by virtue of similar charters
granted after the time by the same king, through
which tolls, dues, and tallages were allowed to be
levied by other towns and communities, the traders
and merchants of Ipswich were placed in precisely
the same situation as other persons who possessed
no royal immunity. It is true that they could not
be fined, nor amerced, except by the laws possessed
by free boroughs, and here, perhaps, they were
placed in a position above a large number of towns,
whose inhabitants, bound down by the most rigid
laws, and existing entirely at the mercy of rapacious
and ignorant feudal chieftains, were little otherwise
than serfs and retainers. This last was a thraldom
of an odious character, from which it was worth
while paying a large sum to be exempt; and though
but a transfer from the rule of the nobles to that of
the monarch, who could always interfere and place
his hand upon the lion's share of any accumulation
of the industrious citizens, yet the knowledge of the
existence of the spoil not being so readily known to
the distant monarch as the neighbouring baron, the
chances were that it rested unmolested from the
grasp of both baronial and regal robber.

From this period it would appear that the town increased in population, and that the numerous transactions incidental to a commercial community, rendered it necessary that courts should be held for the purpose of controlling them. As early as 1254, it is found by the existence of documents, that a Court of Pleas was established in the town for the trial of disputed debts, without the king's writ. The creation of such a court, necessarily arising out of the transactions of a community engaged in trade, is a sufficient proof that the town was progressing in importance as a place of commerce.

The town of Ipswich being remotely situated from the great lines of communication through the heart of the kingdom, was rendered comparatively exempt, by her isolated situation, from the storms of battle and desolation, which at this early period frequently passed over the more internal parts of England. The town, however, in conjunction with the neighbouring part of the country, espoused in a degree the cause of the sons of Henry the Second against their father. During the unnatural contest waged between the parties, a large army of Flemings, headed by Robert de Bellomont, the brave Earl of Leicester, sailed up the Orwell and landed at this port. From thence they passed to Framlingham castle, the strong-hold of Hugh Bigod, who, with several of the neighbouring chieftains, upheld the power of the princes against the monarch, their father. The authorities into whose hands the custody of the town of Ipswich was at the time committed, repelled the force of Leicester with all the power their feeble garrison could muster. The wild valour, however, of an army brought to the shores of a foreign country for the purpose of carrying on an exterminating warfare would not, it must naturally be supposed, allow the scanty garrison of a sea-port town to offer any effectual opposition to their designs. A fierce attack was made upon the castle of Ipswich and the structure was demolished by the Flemings. The Flemings afterwards, attacked the castle of Haugh-ley, commanded by Ralph Broc, for the king, and razed it to the earth. Continuing such excesses as these, the Flemings at length, flushed with victory, passed across the county of Suffolk from Framling-ham to Fornham St. Genovieve, where they were met by the king's party, who had gathered a large force under Henry de Bohun, at Bury St. Edmund's, and after a savage encounter were completely routed. Ten thousand of the Flemish army are said to have fallen upon this occasion. The dead are buried beneath barrows standing near the village of Fornham, a few miles from the town of Bury St. Edmund's, in the western division of the county.*

The date of the battle is 1173, and it completely destroyed the hopes of the rebels in this part of the country. At the close of the contest, the king ordered all castles which had either harboured the

* Some authorities contend that the Earl and his army disembarked at Walton, in Suffolk.

friends of his sons, or contributed in any way to the carrying on of the struggle, should be destroyed. Several castles in the county of Suffolk were in consequence dismantled and thrown down. Walton castle, which had rendered good service to the insurgents, shared the allotted fate of demolition, and the stones of which its walls were composed were scattered through the adjacent villages, and used by the villagers in the construction of roads and cottages.

Of the building occupied as a place of strength, and called by the title of the castle of Ipswich, no remains exist, either to record its situation, or the era in which it was erected. The town still possesses a kind of half fosse known by the name of the "ditches," which might either have belonged to a building of military strength, or to the defensive walls of the place. Whether, however, the spot occupied by this fosse was in ancient times the locality of a fortress, or not, is equally unknown, and most probably will for ever remain so.

The long devastating wars between Henry and his sons had, to a certain degree, paralysed the efforts of the inhabitants of the kingdom to follow out a course of emulation and rivalry, which had sprung up not only in the manufacture of various species of fabric which had found favour in the kingdom, but also with foreigners themselves. A growing intercourse with the continent, had made the English acquainted with the productions and industrial inventions of other nations, and they followed them

with all the ardour of novelty, and the zeal of a
people determined to become acquainted with the
riches of their neighbours. The Flemings, spared
from the wreck of Leicester's army, glad to purchase
their lives and subsistence by locating among their
conquerors, were anxious to conciliate, and change
their past enemies into present friends, by imparting
to them the secrets and peculiarities of their own
clever handicrafts. War and pillage, however, had
depressed and diverted the powers of the people to
better their own uncivilized condition; nor was it
until years had healed the breaches of internal warfare, and cast down the obstacles of partizanship,
that the nation emerged from a state of stagnation
to that of progress.

Ipswich, at this period a small port of trade, especially felt the depressing influences of the wars of
Henry. Hordes of Flemings, incited to join their
brethren, who had gone before them in obtaining
such spoil as the warfare in a new and comparatively
rich country would, in their opinion, inevitably
furnish, constantly found their way up the stream of
the Orwell, and joined their countrymen, located in
the surrounding country from the town of Ipswich.
Bands of these lawless men ravaged the neighbourhood, laying waste the crops, and burning the
habitations of the people. Only a few miles distant,
existed the vast camp and stronghold of Leicester
himself;* from whence, when the vigilance of his
enemies was remitted, he came forth to ruin the

* Framlingham castle.

entire county with fire and sword. Added to this,
a large force belonging to the king was stationed at
Bury St. Edmund's, which harrassed the country
around, and saved the lives and properties of the
subjects of the realm by an interference which
differed but little from an offensive attack. All
these depressing influences tended to injure and
retard the otherwise rising trade of the port. Time,
by degrees, however, healed the breaches made by
intestine commotion, and Ipswich moved forward
with the tide of improvement which set in upon
the nation at large, to a better and a more important
condition.

It may safely be presumed that the increased
commerce and population of the place, induced
John to grant, by purchase, a charter to the inhabitants of Ipswich, the particulars of which have
just been mentioned.

The commotions arising out of the quarrels
between John and his barons, do not appear to
have engaged the attention of Ipswich to any
remarkable extent. The merchants probably desirous to consolidate their trade and place it upon a
firm basis, paid more attention to the attractions of
commerce than to the collisions of refractory feudal
chieftains with a wicked and perfidious monarch.
And where the king, who weighed with the most
scrupulous care the probabilities of exacting gold,
without much opposition, from the coffers of his
subjects, thought he could do so unchecked,
favoured the designs and wishes of the merchants

with regard to the extension of their own designs.
Profuse of words, he promised all things, from
general immunities or freedom, down to personal
exemptions. He caused it to be made known that
he would protect all foreign merchants who should
come to the kingdom, to the same extent as English-
men, and that the laws of the nation should consider
them equal with subjects of the realm. For the
purpose of making known his intention in this
matter, he caused general letters of information to
be dispatched to several of the maritime counties
and towns. Among the former was Suffolk, and
among the latter Ipswich. These letters were not
distributed more northerly than the county of
Norfolk, from which circumstance it is thought
that the principal maritime counties and seaports
did not extend themselves beyond that point.
John, however, though perfectly ready to issue an
immunity, did not generally feel disposed to do so
without receiving value in return, more than amply
rewarding him for his trouble and royal condescension. In the seventh year of his reign, he levied a
tax called " quinzieme," a tallage or excise on merchants, apparently for the exigencies of the state,
but in reality for the purpose of filling his own
empty coffers. With the towns that contributed
to the tax, are to be found Ipswich, Dunwich, and
Orford, the amount levied on Ipswich being nearly
£300. per annum. The richer trades of London
contrived to purchase their freedom from this impost by the payment of a sum in ready money, less

than the amount of the tax for a year—to such shifts
was the monarch at times reduced, to raise supplies
for the purposes of his own designs upon the instant.
Ipswich continued to pay the tax yearly.

There are but few notices of the actual condition
of the trade and commerce of this early time, connected with Ipswich and its locality, that have come
down to us. In the year 1213, however, the fifteenth
year of the reign of John, it is found that Ipswich,
in connexion with the other ports of Suffolk, paid
as the amount of duty levied on woad, used for
dyeing purposes, the sum of £50. Towards this
impost, the ports of Yorkshire paid £96, the ports
of Lincoln £47, Southampton £72. A comparison
of these sums with that paid by the Suffolk ports,
puts us at once into possession of the comparative
amount of commerce between Ipswich and other
places.

From this period onward, for more than a
century, there is little to record with reference to
Ipswich, but the establishment within it of several
monastical institutions, whose existence arose out
of that wide spread of religious feeling, which soon
instituted a powerful domestic tyranny throughout
the land. The annals of the commerce of the place
are but scattered and minute. The town, however,
was doubtless devoted to trade. Its proximity to
the shores of the European continent, in those earlier
periods of our history, when the connection, either
by war or peace, between this county and Europe
might be almost said to be constant, its inhabitants

could not by possibility be excluded from entering upon mercantile affairs. The history of the trade of the nation, therefore, when in the reigns of Richard the Second and Henry the Fourth it became increased to a large extent, will afford us a fair insight into the condition of the town.

One of the earliest monasteries established in Ipswich was that of Trinity or Christ church. It was situated near the site of the present St. Margaret's church, and dates its origin previously to the year 1177.

The establishment was that of a community of Augustine canons, " founded or chiefly endowed by Norman Gastrode fil. Eadnothe, Ernoldus, and Fulco, canons here, and Simon fil. Osberni." The monks appear to have been driven from their convent by a conflagration, but they were reinstated in their possessions by John de Oxford, bishop of Norwich, previously to the year 1200. The community was not large, as at the dissolution of monasteries the convent was found to accommodate only a prior and six or seven canons. The value of the possessions appear according to Tax. Eccle. 1291, £47. 17s. 4½d.—according to Valor Ecclesiasticus, 1534, the clear value of £88. 6s. 9d.—by Liber Val, the gross value of £119. 16s. 2d. These sums were derived from the advowsons, and portions of the churches of St. Lawrence, St. Mary at Tower, St. Mary at Elms, St. Savoir, St. John Baptist, St. Margaret, Trinity, and St. Michael in the borough of Ipswich. In other parts of the county, the

c

convent possessed property at Tudenham, Morning-thorpe, Mendham, Rushmere, Foxhall, Bentley, Higham, Willisham, and Preston. It also owned a water course, and a mill in Hagonford—pasturage for four hundred sheep, free warren in eleven parishes, and rents in many other places. In the year 1203 John gave a charter to this monastery.

Christ church was one of the monasteries given to Cardinal Wolsey, for the endowment of his colleges. This property afterwards passed into the hands of Sir Thomas Pope. The rectory and advowson of the vicarage was granted to Lionel Tolmache, in 1544.

The site of the convent is now the property of W. C. Fonnereau, Esq. A spacious mansion is erected where stood the ancient monasterial edifice, and a park of circumscribed dimensions, but containing very fine timber, and of general beauty, surrounds it. The estate is called after the name of the olden establishment—Christ church.

Previously to 1199, a hospital for lepers was established in the town, as we find that king John granted a fair to be held on the "morrow of St. James the Apostle" for its support. There are no remains of this establishment left. At the dissolution its revenues were annexed to the rectory of St. Helen.

The third monastical establishment in Ipswich was the Priory of St. Peter and St. Paul, situate near the present St. Peter's church. It was of the order of Augustine canons.

GATEWAY OF WOLSEY'S COLLEGE, IPSWICH.

It was upon the ruin of this priory that Cardinal Wolsey founded his college, and as both the history of the founder, and the college itself form a part of the history of Ipswich, it is necessary to enter minutely into the particulars of both.

On proceeding from Lower Brook street, through College street, in the direction of St. Peter's church, the attention of the stranger is attracted towards an ancient brick-built gateway standing on the right. This erection is all that now remains of the college built by Cardinal Wolsey, in and for the benefit of his native town. This gateway cannot be supposed to have been the principal entrance to so magnificent a structure as the college is supposed to have been, but only an outlet from a wing or inferior portion of the edifice, nevertheless it must ever be viewed with interest, being all that Time and an angry despot have left us of this once noble endowment. The church, dedicated to St. Peter, stands a little beyond the gateway, and is supposed, though not on good authority, to have been the place of worship appointed for the members of the college. As a building it possesses no architectural attractions, being of inconsiderable magnitude, and very plain. The font alone is curious from its antiquity, and the grotesque decorations with which it is covered.

It is now clearly proved that Wolsey first drew breath in a house situate in St. Nicholas street, on the south-side of the passage leading into St. Nicholas churchyard, and now occupied by Mr.

Cowell, surgeon. This event took place in March, 1471. There still exists much controversy among the learned as to the station in life held by Wolsey's parents. One of his early biographers, affirms that he was, " a man undoubtedly born to honor ; some prince's bastard, no butcher's son." Fiddes also contradicts the opinion current in his time of his being a butcher's son, and says that his father was the owner of an estate, the value of which was for those times very considerable. Several other authorities agree that " the Cardinal's father was a respectable *grazier* in the town of Ipswich, and not a poor butcher." We must remember that Wolsey had many friends, whose interest and pleasure it was to leave nothing untried that could tend towards the advantage of their patron ; and also many enemies who anxiously sought every means to disparage and injure his reputation. These last persist that he was of lowly origin, and endeavour to support their assertion by reference to the arms of the Cardinal, as represented on the windows of Christ Church College, Oxford, which are surmounted, as they affirm, by a dog gnawing the " spade bone" of a shoulder of mutton. There remains little doubt but that Wolsey's father erected the meat shambles in this town, and that a head, representing either himself or his son, was placed over the entrance. This, however, is no more a proof of Wolsey's father being a butcher, than that those persons who project or build market halls in the present day, should by posterity be thought to have traded in the market. All these real or supposed disadvantages could not, however, obscure or conceal from even the enemies of Wolsey that true nobility, greatness of mind, and talent, which all were compelled to own united in the person of this great man.

"Great Priest! whoever was thy sire by kind,
    Wolsey of Ipswich ne'er begot thy mind!"

It will be seen upon a slight review of this vexed question, that the reason for supposing Wolsey's father to have been a butcher rests upon little or no foundation. Smollet, the historian, seems only to have followed the current opinion of the writers of his time, in stating the received opinion, and to have neglected any research after authorities which would have given him better information. The enemies of the Cardinal encouraged the notion of his low birth, and made the most injurious uses of the report.

In the second volume of Edmondson's Heraldry, the arms of Wolsey are emblazoned, and a naked arm embowed, holding a shin bone, all proper, is used as the crest.

Wolsey's parentage may now, however, be put aside. Returning to his early life, we find that on being sent to school, he manifested so much talent, and industry, that either his father or his friends supplied the means for sending him to college at Oxford, in order to educate him for the priesthood. We have no information relative to any particular person who assisted Wolsey in his

preparatory studies, and as the learning allowed
beyond the cloister was then limited, we may
suppose that the difficulties attendant on the attainment of knowledge, gave rise to the wish of smoothing the way to other youthful aspirants, and induced
him to make the first use of his power by founding
a college, in which the young men of his native
town might receive that assistance which he had
himself needed.

The exact date of Wolsey's entrance at Magdalen
college is not ascertained; but as he took his
degree of bachelor in 1485, it might bring the date
of his matriculation to 1483, allowing him to have
pursued his studies for two years previously. By
this we find he was only twelve years old when he
went to Oxford.

It is most probable that Wolsey did not return to
Ipswich until his father's death, which took place
in October, 1496. During this period, his many
and great capabilities had begun to distinguish him
from others of his contemporaries. He was already
a fellow of his college, and considered by that body
as the most proper person to be placed at the head
of their most important school. Hither came the
two sons of the Marquis of Dorset, and his patronage
procured for Wolsey the living of Lymington. His
conduct here having made him amenable to the law,
he began to find that the obscurity of a country life
was ill suited to his disposition and habits. He
therefore procured the situation of chaplain to the
treasurer of Calais. Here he was introduced to the

notice of Bishop Fox, who soon found means of recommending him to Henry the Seventh. His learning, activity, and aptitude for business, established him in the king's favor, which he retained until his death, and succeeded to a place in the confidence of Henry's son and successor—Henry the Eighth.

The death of Wolsey's father brings us again to the question of his station in life. His will dated September 31st, 1496, devises the whole of his real property to his wife. It is a singular circumstance that the name of Wolsey's parent is in this document spelt *Wuley*, which has naturally led some to suppose that it is the testament of another person. Fiddes, one of the best informed of the early writers on Wolsey's biography, says that the same objection was made in his time to the validity of the instrument; but the dispute was silenced by showing that two instruments despatched from Rome to the younger Wolsey, contain the name spelt as in the father's will—*Wuley.* We subjoin the will for the satisfaction of our readers.

" In Dei Nomine." Amen. September 31st, the year of our Lord God MCCCCLXXXXVI. I, Robert Wuley, of Ippyswiche, whole of mind, and in good memory being, make my testament and last will in this made wise. First, I bequeath my soul to Almighty God, our Lady St. Mary, and to all the company of heaven, and my body to be buried in the churchyard of our Lady St. Mary of Newmarket. Also, I bequeath to the high altar of

St. Nicholas, of Ippyswiche, eleven shillings and eight pence. Also, I bequeath to the painting of the Archangel forty shillings. Item, I will that if Thomas my son be a Priest within a year next after my decease, I will that he sing for me and my friends, by the space of a year, and he to have for his salary ten marks ; and if the said Thomas be not a Priest, I will that another honest Priest sing for me and for my friends for the term aforesaid, and he to have the salary of ten marks. Item, I will that Joan, my wife, have all my lands and tenements in the parish of St. Nicholas, in Ippyswiche aforesaid, and all my free and bond lands, in the parish of St. Stoke, to give and to sell. The residue of my goods not bequeathed, I give and bequeath to the good disposition of Joan my wife, Thomas my son, and Thomas Cady, who I order and make my executors to dispose for me as they shall think best to please Almighty God and benefit my soul—and of this my testament and last will I order and make Richard Farrington supervisor, and he to have for his labour, 13s. 6d.; and if the said Richard deserve more, he for to have more of Joan my wife. Item, I bequeath to the said Thomas Cady, my executor aforesaid, 13s. 3d."

It might easily be inferred from this document that the Cardinal's father was a man of property, by the mention made of lands and tenements both in the town and neighbourhood. We may also suppose that whatever might have been his trade or occupation, he followed none at the time of his death, as

no directions are given as to the disposal of stock
in trade, money in capital, or effects of business.
Though this document may not tend to exalt Wolsey's birth and original station, it proves that he
owed none of his greatness to parental kindness.
The only bequest, and that a trifling one, was con-
tingent upon his becoming a priest within a year,
and performing masses for the repose of his father's
soul. There also appears a deficiency in not appor-
tioning to Wolsey any remuneration for the office of
executor, though the other is expressly provided
for. It may be urged that the station Wolsey then
held in his college rendered the means that his
father could leave him, of little or no value; but as
his becoming a priest appears to have been uncertain, we may presume that he had not then
attained to the high honors which afterwards were
bestowed upon him. All these circumstances seem
to make the whole question very perplexing, and
inclines us the more readily to exclaim with the
old author before quoted, that he was indeed
"some prince's bastard, no butcher's son."

The period now approached when Wolsey, having
attained the summit of wealth and power, resolved
upon putting in execution those plans, by which he
hoped to perpetuate his memory in his native town,
and assist and reform learning. This he intended
accomplishing by the establishment of colleges,
both at Ipswich and Oxford.

But vain are the hopes of the most subtle and
profound! History now begins to show us the

commencement of Wolsey's decline from the favor of his king. It had long been evident to the people that the king's rapacity and extortion were encouraged by Wolsey's misrepresentations. He persuaded Henry that the nation was rich and contented, when at the same time he knew that the commonalty had every reason to be dissatisfied, and that the people generally were both poor and wretched. The princely style of living in which the Cardinal had long indulged, the interfering disposition he manifested in the affairs of foreign nations, and his arrogant and despotic temper, deservedly drew from all ranks the most constant and severe remarks. There is every reason to believe, that the strength of mind with which Wolsey was in a pre-eminent degree endowed, enabled him to overlook the dazzling atmosphere by which he was surrounded, and penetrating into the distant future, perceive that his popularity and power were on the wane. These circumstances urged him the more speedily to complete the establishments he contemplated, in order that by conferring on the nation so great a benefit, he might have a claim on its gratitude. Orders for the suppression of monasteries, and grants giving him the unlimited control over their possessions, were now therefore obtained from the king, even at the most unpropitious times; and it seemed as though they were conferred more to be freed from the importunities of the falling favorite, than from any real sentiment of affection or esteem towards the object or the man.

It is probable that Wolsey had arranged his plans, with regard to the college in this town, before the year 1524, though he found himself unable to put them in execution until 1528. Wolsey had for many years been desirous to see the system of education pursued at this period, thoroughly reformed and amended, the learning which was to be obtained being comparatively useless and superficial. He was determined that at the collegiate school of Ipswich, and also at the more complete establishment in Oxford, a new plan should be pursued in the education of youth, and a sound foundation of pure classical learning laid, to the entire destruction of those " absurd sciences which tended not to make a man learned, but only pert, vain, and shallow." That Wolsey acted upon his object, is proved by the attention he paid to the discipline of the school at Ipswich, and by the care with which he selected the books intended for the use of the students.

An establishment somewhat similar to this can be traced to have existed in Ipswich as far back as the reign of Henry the Second, founded by the " ancestors of Thomas de Lacy and his wife ;" it was however more of an exclusively religious kind. By some authorities the date of this priory has been extended as far back as the conquest, and even beyond that time. It appears to have had many and great benefactors.

At the time of Wolsey's foundation, the revenues were increased so much that the foundation was considered in every way eligible for his purpose.

For many years the various monastic establishments of the kingdom had accumulated to themselves the greater part of the wealth and property of the country; this the king now resolved upon transferring to his own coffers, thereby humbling the excessive pride of the clergy, striking a decisive blow at the bad system these establishments fostered, and also enriching himself. In these matters it is a subject of dispute as to what share the Cardinal had in opposing or assisting the wishes of his royal master. To Wolsey is given all the praise, or all the blame, of the suppression of the monasteries, by some historians; while by others, the excessive rapacity of Henry is made the main spring of action.

That Wolsey's thirst for ecclesiastical power and pomp was excessive is not to be denied. Of this we have sufficient proof in the earnest endeavours he used to be chosen Pope; and also in forming the Legantine Court in England, which was an arbitrary stretch of power, till then unknown to the half-formed constitution of these realms. Notwithstanding the attempts made by this court to extirpate "the Lutheran heresy," it yet did unconsciously promote the advancement of the reformed religion by showing the enormities existing in monastic houses. However this can hardly palliate the many and serious objections that could justly be urged against this court.

It appears somewhat singular that the college at Ipswich should not have been decided upon until that at Oxford was begun, although it is evident that at the former place those studies were to be commenced, which should afterwards be more fully completed at the latter. The reason of this appears to be, that the grant for the suppression of St. Frideswide's monastery at Oxford, was obtained from the king sometime previous to the grants for the support of Ipswich. Some authorities think that this circumstance was accidental. Hall, from the words "this seeson," seems to imply that both these institutions were decided upon at the same time, provided we take the expression "this seeson" to imply a precise point of time. The means employed by Wolsey to support these establishments do him but little credit in the opinion of posterity, and are differently related by Hall. He says, "this seeson the Cardinal beyng in the Kynge's favor, obtained license to make a College at Oxford, and another at Ipswyche; *and because* he would geve no landes to the said Colleges, he obtained of the Bishop of Rome, license to suppresse and put down diverse abbayes, priories and monasteries, to the number of   wherfor sodainly he entered by his commissioners into the said houses and put out the religious, and tooke all their goodes and moveables, and scarcely gave the poore wretches any thyng, except it were to the heddes of the house; and then he caused thexcheter to sit, and to finde the house voyde, relynquished, and founde the

Kyng founder, when other men wer founders, and
with thes landes he endowed all his colleges, which
he *begun so sumptuous*, and the scholars wer so
proude that everie persone judged that they would
not be good."

Wolsey now eagerly hastened to possess himself
of the riches of those monasteries, the dissolution
of which he had decided upon. Numerous are the
stories related of the means by which he compassed
his designs. It is told, that seeking to gain possession of the monastery of Daventry, he sent five
persons to negotiate the business with the head of
that community. After some discussion, the demand
was firmly denied. This Wolsey's agents affected
greatly to resent, and thereby raised a quarrel and
disturbance; whereupon Wolsey caused the establishment to be dissolved and the revenues added
to those already devoted to the maintenance of his
new colleges. This outrage was asserted to have
been severely visited by Providence upon the persons of the five agents for the part they took in
these affairs. Two of them quarrelling, one was
killed, and the other suffered the extreme penalty
of the law. Another accounted in those days a rich
man, in three years became so poor as to be obliged
to beg his bread for the remainder of his life. The
fourth drowned himself; while the principal actor in
this work of destruction "was cruelly maimed in
Ireland, even at such time as hee was a bishop."
This person's name was Dr. Allen.*

* Historic Sites of Suffolk, p. 75.

The priory of St. Peter's, Ipswich, was yielded to the Cardinal on the 6th of March, 1527; William Brown being at that time Prior; and on the 15th of June, 1528, the first stone of the college was laid by John Longland, Bishop of Lincoln, in the presence of a large concourse of spectators. The building rapidly progressed, and the corporation displayed the interest they felt in this acquisition to the town, by bestowing upon it the lands bequeathed to them by Richard Felawe, lying at Whitton and in the town of Ipswich.

This act of the municipal authorities is duly enrolled in the great Court Book of the Corporation, where it is specified that, at an assembly of the Bailiffs, Portmen, Commonalty, and Burgesses, held on the Wednesday next, after the Feast of the Nativity, in the 20th year of the reign of King Henry the Eighth, (1528,) present:—

James Hill, Thomas Manser, } Bailiffs	Thomas Barbor Robert Babett
Humphrey Wingfield, Esq.	Alexander Spyhawke
Lionel Talmage, Esq.	William Ligy
Henry Stannard	William Stanner
John Butteler	Richard Coppynge
Robert Daundy	Thomas Sely
James Kirby	John Alin
Robert Grey	Thomas Reyson
Robert Toyner	John Weste, (Saddler)
John Pypho	Walter Gowty
William Revet	Thomas Ware, (Smyth)
Thomas Mellys	John Cowper, (Mercer)
Thomas Cuttyng	Robert Spillynge
John Barker	William Gregory
Matthewe Woode	Thomas Ptyrrolle
John Pitman	John Maye
Christopher Heywarde	Thomas More, (Mercer)
Edward Bettes	William Stanner, jun.

—the Bailiffs, Portmen and Burgesses, by unanimous assent and consent, give and grant and con-
vey to the Dean and Canons of the Cardinal's
College of the Blessed Mary the Virgin, in the
said Town of Ipswich, all the right and interest
which they have in certain Lands, Tenements, and
Appurtenances, in Ipswich and Whitton, according to the last Will of Richard Felawe, late of the
said Town of Ipswich, Merchant.

It is not possible at the present day to enumerate
all the sources from which the revenues of the
college were derived. We have before stated that
the valuation of the priory itself in Taxatio Ecclesiastica, date 1291, was £46. 0s. 11d. This
included possessions in 54 parishes. Holding the
manors of Harrold in Burstall, St. Peter in Cre-
tingham, and Hintlesham ; also the tithes of St.
Matthew's, Ipswich, Letheringham, Thorpe, &c.
the impropriation of the churches of Crewe,
Wherstead, Dokesworth, St. Austen, St. Mildred,
St. Edmund a Pountney, St. Clement, St. Mary at
the Key, St. Peter, and some others, it is probable
that its revenues at the time of its suppression for
the purposes of Wolsey were considerably beyond
the sum above mentioned.

Beyond the possessions of this priory, Cardinal
Wolsey caused the suppression of the following
religious houses, and bestowed their property upon
the college.—

DODNASH, a priory of Augustines, or Black
Canons, dedicated to St. Mary, founded at an early

era by the ancestors of the Earls of Norfolk. It held the tithe of barley in Fakenham, in Colneis : 320 acres of land in Hemingstone and Coddenham ; 320 acres in Burstall and Bramford ; a house and 39 acres of land in Bergholt ; and free warren, lands, and rents, in 15 parishes. Its valuation in 1291, was £19. 19s. 5d., and according to Dugdale and Speed, £42. 18s. 8½d. Date of its suppression, 1524.

FELIXSTOW, a small cell dedicated to St. Felix, and founded by Roger Bigod, first Earl of Norfolk. Its valuation, in Tax. Eccles., £6. 16s. 1d.

RUMBURGH, an ancient priory, founded between 1064 and 1070 by the Monks of the Abbey of Hulme. It was a cell and priory, dedicated to St. Michael or St. Felix, and was valued in Taxatio Ecclesiastica at £10. 12s. 11¾d. Date of grant to Wolsey 1528.

WYKES, a small hospital, believed to have been stationed in Cambridgeshire. Its revenue was very small. Date of suppression not known.

SNAPE, a priory of Benedictine Monks, founded in 1099 by William Martel, his wife, and sons, to the use of which they gave the manor of Snape. The benefit of all wrecks of the sea from Thorp to Orford Ness was also conferred upon it. Originally attached to the convent of St. John of Colchester, the priory underwent before its suppression a change of masters, rather unusual with property of this description. Founded in 1099—occupied in 1155—a cell to Colchester till 1403, then conven-

tual until 1508—a cell to Butley until 1509, and a
second time conventual until 1524; it then fell into
the hands of Wolsey. Its endowments included the
churches of Aldeburgh, Friston, and Bedingfield;
and the several manors of Bedingfield, Snape,
Friston, Aldeburgh, Scotts, and Tastard's. Its
value in Tax. Eccles., in thirteen parishes, was
£32. 12s. 7½d. According to Dugdale, £99. 1s. 11½d.
and in the Valor Ecclesiasticus, 1534, to the
same amount. The date of its suppression,
1524.

MOUNTJOY, a priory of Austin Canons, situated
in the hundred of Eynsford, Norfolk. It was
founded by William de Gyney, about the reign of
Richard the First or King John. It held peculiar
privileges—among them the right of celebrating
divine service during interdict, and all who should
hold unlawful possession of its revenues were sen-
tenced to excommunication. The rectories of
Stanfield, Irmingland, and Heverland were appropriated to its use. The valuation in Tax. Eccles.
was only £2. 0s. 7¼d., but it afterwards rose to a
high amount. It was suppressed, and its revenues
given to Ipswich college, in 1528.

BROMHILL, a priory and conventual church of
Austin Canons, situated in the hundred of Grim-
shoe, Norfolk, founded in the reign of John or
Henry the Third, by Sir Hugh de Plais, and dedi-
cated to the Blessed Virgin and St. Thomas the
Martyr, Archbishop of Canterbury. Value in Tax.
Eccles., in Norfolk, £23. 8s. 2d., and Suffolk,

£2. 2s. 7d. Suppressed in 1528, at which period seven manors were in its possession.

BLIBURGH, a priory of Augustine Canons, was also suppressed by bull for the purposes of Ipswich college; but its revenues were never attached. It would have formed a very considerable addition to the possession of that establishment had its annexation been concluded. This was also a very ancient foundation, the church of Bliburgh having been presented to the priory by Henry the First. It was dedicated to the honour of the Blessed Virgin Mary, and its value, according to Tax. Eccles. in Suffolk, 37 parishes, £32. 18s. 2½d.; in Norfolk, £1. 6s. Valor Ecclesiasticus, 1534, £48. 8s. 10d.—gross value by the same authority, £60. 13s. 4d.

Trinity, or Christ Church Priory, at Ipswich, was also given to Wolsey for his college. Value, Tax. Eccles. £47. 17s. 4½d.; Valor Eccles.; clear value £88. 6s. 9d.; gross value £119. 16s. 2d. This establishment stood near the present mansion of Christ Church, the property of the Rev. C. Fonnereau.

The revenues of Horkesley, and Tiptree Priory, in Essex.

A portion of the possessions of Wendling, in Norfolk, granted for the endowment of both colleges.

According to Howard, it appears also that the rectory of Marybone, after being appropriated to the Dean and Canons of Christ Church, was at their request granted to the masters and scholars of the School of Ipswich.

Such were the revenues of Wolsey's College, as
collected from many sources, bearing the stamp of
authority.   It is not improbable that other gifts
were bestowed by the generous founder upon the
object of his care and attention, but of which record
is lost, or difficult to discover.   The establishment
appears to have met with the warm approbation of
his fellow townsmen, the principal owners of the
soil in the county, and notices are extant of the
feasting on fat bucks, and the distribution of gifts
or money to celebrate its existence.

Although the revenues of the college were ample,
it does not appear to have been overburdened with
servants and retainers.   The foundation consisted
of a dean, eight clerks, twelve secular canons, eight
choristers, and fourteen beadsmen; and we find the
Dean, William Capon, complaining that there was
more than sufficient employment for one individual
as a Sacristan in the church, and praying that other
assistance in that important department of the
Catholic ceremonial might be granted at Wolsey's
earliest convenience, until which time arrangements
had been made to prevent neglect in the duties of
the office.   This dean, the first and last of Ipswich
College, appears to have been a person zealously
attached, not only to the establishment over which
he was appointed to preside, but also to the person
of his munificent master and patron.   The following
letter written by him to Wolsey, and containing
many minor particulars relating to the opening of
the college, displays this feeling in an eminent
degree.

" Pleasith it your Grace to be advertysed, the
Sonday the vjte day of September, maister Stephyns,
Doctor Lee, with Mr. Crumwell, repayred to Gipswiche and came to your Grace's College there, and
brought with theym coopes, vestements, aulter
clothes, plate, and other things, the perticullers
whereof byn comprised in a payer of Indenturs
made bitwene me and the said Mr. Crumwell; the
oon indenture the said Mr. Crumwell hath with
hym and thoder part remeyneth with me.   Also all
the said parcells be ingroced and incerted into your
Graces boke indented, amongst other of your graces
stuff, which boke remeyneth in my custodye.   Also
the said Mr. Stephyns, Mr. Lee, and Mr. Crumwell
taryed in your graces College the space of iiij dayes,
in whiche tyme Mr. Crumwell dyd take moche
payne and labour not only in surveying your graces
stuff hether caryed sawfely, but also in prepayring
and ordering offhangings, benchis, with all other
necessaries to the furniture of our hall whiche ys
now well trymmed and ordered thrugh his good
diligence and helpe.   And upon our Ladyes evyn I,
with all the company of your Grace's college, as the
subdeane, Mr. Ellis, vj. presta, viij. clerks, and ix.
choresters, with all our servants, when we had
fynshed our evynsong in our college chirche, then
immedyatly after we repayred together to our
Ladyes Chapell, and there song evynsong as so-
lemply and devoutely as we cowde.   And there
accompanyed with Mr. Stephyns, Doctor Lee, and
Mr. Crumwell, with Mr. Humphrey Wyngfylde, (to

whom all we of your Grace's college byn moche
boundyn unto for his loving and kynde maner
shewed unto us,) the bayliffs of the towne, with the
port-men and the Priour of Christs Chirche, all the
whiche accompanyed us that same night home
agayne to your Graces college with as lovying and
kynde maner as I have sene ; and at theyr commyng
theder they dranke with me bothe wyne and biere,
and so that nyght departed. On the next Day
whiche was our Ladyes day, the viij. day of September; a day of very fowle wedder and rayned
sore contynewally; so that we cowde not go in
procession thrugh the towne to our Lady's Chapell
accordyng to our statute by your grace made; but
we made as solempe a procession in your grace's
College Chirche as cowde be devysed. In somoche
there were xl. of your coopes worne there, and
asmoche people as cowde stande in the Chirche and
in the chirche yarde. Also all the honnorable
gentilmen of the shyre were there ; as Mr. Wente-
ford, Sir John Willowghbye, Sir Phelip Tylney,
Mr. Bowth, Sir Thomas Tey, with Mr. Benefylde,
Mr. Pyrton, Mr. Jermeyn, Mr. Humfrey Wyngfylde,
with many other to the nomber of xxiiij. gentilmen
of the contrey, besids the bayliffs, porte-men of the
towne, the Priour of Christs Chirche, the Priour of
Butley, Doctor Grene vicar of Alborough, as com-
myssaries bothe to your Grace and to the Bishope
of Norwiche, and the Duke of Norfolk's almoner
Mr. Hege, all the whiche were there, with as good
wille and diligence as they cowde to do your Grace

honnor that day : and they all toke repast at dynner
in your Grace's College, and as I trust wele enterteyned with good fare, and suche fassyon as we
cowde devise, where with they were right well
contented as I supposed. Fardemore as for your
syngyng men byn well chosen, very well brested
with sufficient cunnyng for theyr rowmes, and som
of theym very excellent, whiche will not serve here
with theyr good wills for that wagis, alleging for
theyr selff how they had moche better wages there
from whense they came fro. Moreover they will
have breakfasts every day in as ample and large
manner as they have had in other places. I feare
that theyr commons allowed by your Grace will not
suffice theym as yet : for we can make no provysions
neyther for beeffs ne for muttons for want of pasture
nere unto us. As for Bornebridge ys very bareyne.
The subdeane and I, with Mr. Rushe, have vewed
every part and percell thereof, and they saye it is
not mete nor convenyent for fatte ware, neyther for
beeffs nor muttons. I have enterteyned theym
according to your Graces commandment with good
wordis and plenty of mete and drinke, promysing
to syng to som of theym that be excellent more
wagis, for they gruge sore at theyr wagis, as Mr.
Doctor Stepheyns and Mr. Crumwell can shew to
your Grace more at lengthe. Fardemore as for
your Graces College Churche, oon man ys not able
bothe to attende and kepe the revestry and do all
things in the Churche, as to ryng the bells, kepe
the Churche clene, prepayre the aulter's lights, and

other necessaries, and to see all the Ornaments wele
and sufficiently repayred, and kepte withoute eny
empayring, and to set forth every day all suche
things as is to be occupied abowte Godd's service.
Therefore by the advyce of Mr. Stephyns, Mr. Lee,
and Mr. Crumwell I have putt in to the churche an
other man to helpe the yoman off the Revestry, and
named him Sexton, unto the tyme I knowe farder
of your Grace's pleasure in that behalf. Also here
byn but fyve prestis besids your Subdeane, which is
to litle a nomber to kepe iij. massys every day
according to your Graces statuts, and the subdeane
cannot attende upon his charge for surveyeng of
the works and bieldyngs of your Grace's College,
wherfor we moost humbly desyer and pray your
Grace to have moo priests to performe your Grace's
ordynaunce in your sayd College, or els to dyspense
with us for oon of your masses, eyther the Requiem
Masse or ells our Ladyes masse, unto the tyme we
be better furnished with priests to accomplishe and
performe your Graces ordynaunces and statutes
therein. And but for Mr. Leutall we cowde in a
manner do nothing in our quere. He taketh very
great paynes and is alwaye present at Mattens and
all Masses with evyn song, and settith the quere in
good ordre fro tyme to tyme, and fayleth not at eny
time. He is very sober and discrete, and bringeth
up your Choresters very wele : assuring your Grace
there shall be no better children in no place of
England then we shall have here, and that in short
tyme. I have also made xv. albis of the new cloth

whiche I had of your Grace, delyvered by thandis
of Mr. Alvarde your graces servaunt; and yet there
is xiiij. albis more to be made to the sutes now
lately seut by your Grace to us Mr. Crumwell;
besids albis for xiiij. tunycles, and xij. payer of
odde parrers for children.   Fardermore there hath
byn sent unto your Graces College, agaynste the
day of the Nativitie of our Ladye, ix. bukks; that
is to wete ij. from the Duke of Norfolke, ij. from
the Duke of Suffolke, oon from my Lady of Oxford
the yonger, oon from Sir Phelip Bowth, oon from
Mr. Pryton, oon from Nr. Sentcler your graces
servaunt, and oon from Richard Cavendish your
grace's servaunt; whiche bukks were spent on our
sayd Ladyes day in your Graces College and in the
towne of Gipswiche, whereof oon buk was delyv'ed
to the Chamberleyns of the towne for the xxiiij.
hedmen of the same towne, and in money xs. to
make merry with all, by the advyce of Mr. Stephens,
Mr. Lee, and Mr. Crumwell: and in lyke wise to
the bayliffs wyves and the portemennes wives to
make mery with a buk and xs.   And to the Curatts
of the same towne a buk with vjs. viijd. in money,
for theyr paynes and labowrs takyn in our procession.   Also Mr. Rushe to whom all your Graces
College is moche bedoldyn unto, ever redy to do
pleasurs and also to take paynes for us in all our
causes, and at the sayd day he gave to us vj. cowple
of conyes, ij. fesaunts, and oon dosseyn of quayles.
Also the Priour of Butley he gave to us ii. fesaunts
and a fatte Crane.

"Also we have receyved of Mr. Dawndy clxxj. tonnes of Cane stone, and within a fortenyght next after Mighelmes now next commyng we shall have oon c. tonnes more. So that your workemen shall not be un occupyed for wante of stone. And the sayd Mr. Dawndy hath promised to me that bifore Easter next commyng we shall have here redy Mi. tonnes more of the sayd Cane stone. And thus the Holy Trinitie preserve your Grace. From your Grace's College in Gipswiche the xxvj. day of September, by your most boundyn servaunt and humble Chapleyn." WILLYAM CAPON.

The time now approaches when we must see Wolsey under far different circumstances than those in which we have for so many years been accustomed to contemplate him. He had now arrived at the summit of his worldly greatness, and the covetousness and rapacity he had himself exercised towards others, and fostered in the king, was by that personage directed against his possessions.

One thing after another was given up, and the unhappy Cardinal himself cited to appear before what he too well knew to be an inexorable court. The anxiety of his mind became too great for his enfeebled body to sustain, and he breathed his last at Leicester Abbey, (where he had stopped to rest) on the 30th of November, 1530. Immediately upon his death, the king took possession of all the revenues which had been appropriated to the foundation and maintenance of the college in Ipswich, and scattered them among various per-

sons. Thus by an act of malicious revenge was the
town deprived of a useful and honorable appendage,
and the name and remembrance of Wolsey almost
lost in his native place.

Little now remains to be told concerning the
college. All that is left of the building is the gateway to undoubtedly an inferior part of the edifice.
It was formerly more ornamented than it is at
present; but the pinnacles with which it was
adorned have disappeared, and even the foundation
stone, bearing a commemorative inscription, is
carried away and deposited in the College of Christ
Church, Oxford.

Much research and anxious inquiry has been
made by those interested in such studies concerning
the condition and external appearance of this institution. Their inquiries have ended in disap-
pointment; nothing further being known but that
the whole site comprised as much as six acres; but
what portion of this was occupied by buildings,
cannot be ascertained. Neither does any account
remain of its precise style of architecture; but as
we are aware that Wolsey possessed a profound
knowledge of that science, and a most correct taste,
there is no reason to doubt but that the building,
as far as completed, was indeed "sumptuous to
behold." In the letter from Wm. Capon, dean, to
Wolsey, relative to the progress of the building, we
find him saying, that "we have receyved of Mr.
Dawndy, clxxj. tonnes of cane stone, and within a
fortenyght next after Mighelmes now next comyng,

we shall have oon c. tonnes more. So that your
workemen shall not be un-occupied for wante of
stone. And the sayde Mr. Dawndy hath promised
to me, that bifore Easter next commyng, we shall
have here redy M. tonnes of the sayd cane stone."
If the last numeral is intended to specify a thousand
tons, the quantity required gives us an idea of a
building to be erected on a large scale. Thus it
will be perceived that our best knowledge on this
subject is very imperfect, and it also appears improbable whether any more certain evidence will
ever be obtained.

Various engraved representations of Wolsey's
Gate are in existence. Grose, in his Antiquities,
gives a view;—this, we believe, is one of the
earliest. There is a second representation in " Ex-
cursions through Suffolk." A third appears in
" Ancient Reliques ;" Conder del., Tyrrell engraver.
There is a fourth view in the " History of Ipswich,"
and various others are also extant.

The site passed in 1531 to Thomas Alverde, and
from him to Richard Perceval, and Edmund Duf-
field, in 1611. It is now in possession of the
Messrs. Alexander.

Ipswich possessed also other monastical establishments. One of the most extensive was the
foundation of Black Friars, who settled in the parish
of St. Mary Key, where the " goods of the church"
became exceedingly valuable, and the buildings
extensive. Some of the latter remain even to
the present day.

The Dominican Black Friars, or Friars' Preachers, as they were frequently called, originated in the year A. D. 1206, and made their first appearance in England fourteen or fifteen years after. More than a quarter of a century elapsed previously to the establishment from the great head, settling at Ipswich. To this town, however, they came, and by the liberality of John Harys, erected buildings for the accommodation of their community. Weever, and the historian Speed, say that the Ipswich establishment owes its origin to a trio of worthies, all bearing the christian name of Henry—Henry Redhead, Henry de Manesby, and Henry de Loudham. Whoever might have been the zealous religionist who first raised the order in this town, it is certain that they took for their institution the plot of ground known by the name of the Shire Hall Yard, and erected buildings upon it. Part of these erections are still in being, standing in the left hand side of the area, and used for the purposes of Christ's Hospital Charity, and the Grammar School. The Grammar School, indeed, is held in the very building set apart by the Friars for their refectory, and affords us in the present day a fair idea of the mode and style in which these ancient religious foundations were built, upon the existence of which was thought to depend the very stability of religion itself.

In 1307, the Friars' preachers appear to have accumulated a fund capable of extending the conveniences of their convent, and took occasion immediately upon the accession of Edward the Second to the throne, to obtain from him a patent, or license to extend the precincts of their convent. This work was carried on to a great extent, and the buildings and grounds attached to the institution extended from Star Lane into St. Margaret's parish.

The Friars' preachers continued to grow rich and flourishing, until the remorseless Henry, by his act of dissolution, took the monastic possessions of the kingdom into his own hands. It was afterwards granted to William Sabyn, in 1541, and then purchased by the corporation of Ipswich for the purpose of founding an hospital. This was done, and the establishment took the name of Christ's Hospital, the corporation being secured in their possession by a charter dated in 1572.

There is a building used as a Bridewell upon the site of the monastery, as well as the Hospital itself, and the Grammar-school, in which, some years since, was kept a large collection of printed books, the gift of various individuals to the corporation. These volumes, many of them treating on recondite subjects, and of considerable intrinsic value, were however fast hastening to decay and destruction, as much by the pilfering of the curious and dishonest, as by the effect of damp, when they were removed to the custody of the trustees of the Ipswich Literary Institution, and are now deposited in their apartments in the Town-hall, and freely opened for the use of all respectable applicants. There are many rare volumes among the collection, and much of early divinity and ecclesiastical history.

The monastical establishment had many considerable and noble benefactors. Roger Bigod, Earl Marshall of England, gave largely to the institution, and was placed at his death among its lists of saints or martyrs. It is also recorded that Sir John Sutton, Lady Margaret Plays, Adam de Brandestone, gave of the riches which they possessed to " God's house of the Friars at Ipswich." Robert Ufford, Earl of Suffolk, John Fastolph, and Agnes, his wife, laid their bones beneath its cloisters at their death. Altogether, the convent of the preaching Friars in Ipswich, was of an important character. This, both its history and the remnants of the buildings which time has spared, sufficiently attest.

Another community of Friars—of the order of Carmelites settled, within the present boundaries of the parishes of St. Lawrence and St. Nicholas, in the year 1279. It is not unlikely that this brotherhood were attracted towards a settlement in the town, by the success they had seen attend the brethren of a different order. Lord Bardolph, Sir Jeffery Hadley, Knight, and Sir Robert Norton, were the patrons of the establishment, and under whose protection the possessions of this religious house progressively increased until they became considerable. The establishment was dedicated to St. Mary. At the dissolution, it passed into the possession of John Eyre, and since that period has become, in division, the property of several persons.

The site of the convent was on the spot now called Old Gaol Lane, leading out of the Butter

Market.   Part of the ancient edifice was converted into a gaol under the regulation of the county—hence the name of Gaol Lane.   In the parish of St. Nicholas, the Franciscan Friars had a religious house, founded before 1296, by Sir Robert Tiptot, of Nettlestead, in this county.   It stood a little beyond St. Nicholas' church, to the westward, and a portion of its ruins existed down to within a few years, and may perhaps still exist.   Its dedication was made to St. Francis.   Its site was recently in the possession of Simon Jackaman, Esq.

Besides the religious institutions already enumerated, one or two other similar communities had also establishments within the walls.   They were, however, of minor character· to those mentioned.

It would appear from the number of these religious houses existing at the same time in Ipswich, that a sacerdotal character was thrown over the town, and which probably tended to retard that spirit of enterprise and commerce, which exhibited itself at various periods through the course of years occupied by the duration of their several establishments.   It has been shown by the historians of towns of far greater magnitude than our own, that when filled with monastic institutions, they became retarded in their social energies, and failed to progress in a similar ratio with other places left unencumbered by communities of monks.   We may safely note as a fact, therefore, that had not the various monasteries been established in Ipswich in early times, which she maintained, she would have worked out a character of far greater importance than she bears at the present moment.

We again return to an early era. In 1317, Edward the Second granted a charter to Ipswich, in which the goods and merchandise of its merchants were absolved from the payment of many dues, to which they were subject upon introduction into other ports. Hitherto the town appears to have had four coroners. That number was, by the same charter, reduced to two.

In 1337, Sir John Howard was commissioned and commanded to raise a body of five hundred men to aid in the wars of the king against the French. They were embarked from the port.

In 1328, the second year of Edward the Third, an extensive and powerful fleet of ships of war and merchandise were collected upon the coast of Suffolk, for the purpose of supporting the monarch in his designs upon the kingdom of France.

In 1339, Edward the Third, who was then living at Walton, upon one of his manors, confirmed certain charters which had been granted to Ipswich, and conveyed to it other immunities that the town had not hitherto possessed.

With the exception of a charter granted by Richard the Second, no change of any consequence appears to have been made in the municipality, until the year 1445, when Henry the Sixth incorporates the town under the denomination of " the burgesses of Ipswich." Under the charter conferring this distinction, the bailiffs were empowered

E

to chose four other burgesses, which by some
authorities are considered to have been the commencement of the appointment of assistant magistrates. In the year following, the town chose its
representatives in parliament, although not for the
first time—the corporation paying their expenses
while attending to the onerous duties of their office.
The names of these two ancient worthies were
William Ridout and John Smith.

In 1324, it appears by entries in the patent rolls,
that a great riot broke out in Ipswich, which was
attended with very serious consequences both to
the property and persons of individuals. The
importance of the commotion may be gathered from
the fact that very many influential persons joined in
it. Among these latter were no less than four
individuals, who had all of them at different periods
represented Ipswich in parliament. These legisla-
tive rioters were John Harneys, returned for Ipswich
in the parliament held at York, May 6th, 1319—
Walter Stace, returned in the parliament held at
Westminster, September 23rd, 1313—Thomas
Stace, returned in the parliament held in Westminster, January 20th, 1314—and Gilbert de Burgh,
returned in the parliament held at Westminster,
July 23rd, 1323. These four, together with Philip
Harneys, Henry Stace, Thomas Lee, Thomas le
Maistre, Laurence le Clerk, Simon de Shakelok,
and Hugh, are stated to have raised the tocsin of
opposition to all constituted authorities—to have
compelled others under the influence of fear and

and intimidation, to join them in their lawless projects and excesses, and to have administered to their own followers and certain inhabitants of the town, unlawful and violent oaths. They were further charged with an assault upon Edmund de Castleacre and Gilbert de Burgh, the king's bailiffs of Ipswich, and John Haltebo, constable, while in the exercise of their legitimate offices and duties—attacking them in the house of one John de Preston, where they maimed many persons and committed —so runs the record—other enormous crimes against the authority of their sovereign lord the king.

It is singular that there exists no authentic particulars of the origin or proceedings of this outbreak, which may be considered, from the number of persons implicated—the respectable condition in which they are evidently placed in society—and the nature of the attack, to have been a popular commotion of no common occurrence. As the attack appears to have been directed against the authorities of the king, and the place, it is fair to infer, that the authority of the monarch, as well as that of the municipality, had become the object of violence. Whether it arose out of the quarrel with the D'Espencers, whose cause was one of fruitful jealousy and dissatisfaction throughout the kingdom, or occasioned by some levy made by the king to assist him in his continental wars, is not now known. Whatever might have been the primary cause of the commotion, it evidently was one of a highly important and dangerous nature—sufficient in its consequences to induce the issue of a special commission of Oyer and Terminer for the trial of the delinquents, the date for the holding of which is given in the patent rolls as August 29th, 1324.

It was from the port of Ipswich that the unfortunate, but ambitious William De la Pole, Earl of Suffolk, embarked upon his term of banishment in 1446. The circumstances connected with the career of this nobleman are so closely connected with Suffolk, his vast possessions in the county, and his residence, Wingfield Castle, being within the circle of a pleasant ride from Ipswich—that some part of his history may not inappropriately find a place in this volume.

William De la Pole, Earl of Suffolk, was born in the year ——, and became, when manhood had given him strength and wisdom, a noted warrior in the French wars during the reign of Henry VI. Unfortunately, the celebrated Maid of Orleans made head against the British forces, which were at length driven from the fair fields of France, and the very soil cleared from the presence of its fierce invaders. Previously to these reverses, William De la Pole had raised himself into the position of a chief director of the affairs of the nation, as well as master of the mind and person of king Henry VI. Indeed he governed all. It was Suffolk, who on the desire of Henry, contracted a marriage between him and Margaret of Anjou, the daughter of the titular monarch of Sicily and Jerusalem, and cousin of the French queen. This transaction raised the popular cry against Suffolk, as instead of demanding a dowry from the parent of the princess, he gave up the provinces, Maine and Anjou, to her family—the hereditary possessions of Margaret's father it is true, but at the same time, part of the conquests of the English in France, costing the nation much blood and treasure in capture. The people accused Suffolk of bribery in the transaction; but Henry, pleased with the new toy procured for him, advanced the Earl to the rank of Marquis. Some historians relate, that there existed between Margaret and Suffolk an early attachment of a delicate nature, which would, if true, at least account for some of the events that followed. No sooner were the espousals of Henry with the princess concluded, than a close communication was observed between the queen and Suffolk. It is said they were constantly together, and that he looked more like her husband and king of England, than the unfortunate Henry. She began to govern, and Suffolk assisted her by all means at his disposal—so that in the course of a short space, the weak monarch held no power over his kingdom but in name, and was even content to guide the vessel of the state by the commands and inducements of the queen's party, with Suffolk and Cardinal Beaufort at its head.

Amid the turmoil of faction, now driving the people to the verge of hatred and despair, Humphrey Duke of Gloster—surnamed the " good"— stood up for the supremacy of the king, and the common good of the nation. He, however, was soon made to feel the withering effects of that tyranny which aimed at the absorption of all power into itself. At an earlier period of his life, Gloster had taken one Eleanor Cobham for his mistress—a woman of surpassing beauty and high endowments. He afterwards married her. When she became his duchess, considering that her husband, being the king's uncle, stood next to the crown, she became ambitious, and being desirous of knowing by means of divination when the king would die, she consulted the astrologers of the time, and among other "cunning persons" a woman named Margaret de Jourdain, the witch of Eye. This circumstance becoming known immediately after a quarrel between her husband and the Beaufort party, the duchess was accused of sorcery, enchantment, and with conspiring to destroy the king's body and setting up her husband upon the throne of the realm. One of the crimes attempted to be proved against Alice Cobham was, that she kept a waxen figure bearing the likeness of the king—which in proportion as it was sweated and melted before a flame, would by magical sympathy, cause the flesh and spirit of the king to waste in like manner. On charges such as these she was condemned to perform penance, and to pass the remainder of her life a close prisoner in the Isle of Man, under the custody of one of the Stanley family. The witch of Eye was burnt at Smithfield, and Roger Bolingbroke, a learned astrologer, who it was said aided the intentions of the duchess, was drawn and quartered on the same spot. This was the first great blow aimed at the opposing power of Humphrey Duke of Gloster, by the Suffolk party. The second was the murder of the Duke himself. For this purpose a parliament was convened at Bury St. Edmund's, to which Gloster was invited, where, surrounded by his enemies, a dispute was created to inveigle him into their hands. The base act was accomplished, and he was finally murdered in his bed within the confines of St. Saviour's Monastry, the ruins of which now stand at the end of Northgate Street, in that town. Suffolk, by the popular voice, was denounced as his murderer.

No sooner had the victim to De la Pole's passionate ambition met his fate, than the murderer seized upon his possessions, and, tyrant-like, glutted himself with the rich spoils of his enemy.

An end, however, to Suffolk's guilty course was fast approaching. Fresh disasters, which had been long ripening, broke out upon the continent. The English arms were worsted in France, and the French people became greatly victorious. The heritage of Acquitaine was lost by England, and all that remained offering allegiance to its power, were the citadel and tour of Calais, with the adjoining marshes, commanded by its cannon. Misfortune of all kinds now fell on the minister and nation. The people at length rose against De la Pole, now made Duke of Suffolk, and he sunk beneath the combination of opposing nobles, who sided with the populace. The cry of the whole land went up against the author of the evil. The commonalty appealed to the Commons, and that House demanded, that the Lords should send the delinquent —the man who had brought dishonour and ruin upon the land—to the dungeons of the Tower. An impeachment was preferred against him, charging him with misprision of treason, and waste of the public money. The proceedings on this matter were irregular, and concluded in nothing. A second charge was, however, made against him, which ended in a sentence of banishment, for the space of five years. Suffolk yielded to the rod, and after a public profession of innocence to his retainers upon his estates, he embarked from Ipswich for the continent. Having made way down the channel—near Dover his vessel was brought up by the " Nicholas of the Tower," an English ship of war, of great strength. Ordered on board, his reception from the commander was in the following significant words—" Welcome traitor ;" and after being kept a close prisoner a few days, while communications passed between the captain and the shore, he was conveyed into a cock-boat alongside, on the gunwale of which he was desired to lay his head, and having done so, it was struck from his body at one blow. His remains were afterwards sent for interment in the collegiate church of Wingfield.

The day on which this proud nobleman lost his head was the second of May, 1449.

William De la Pole left behind him possessions

equalling in extent the riches of the most wealthy. In Suffolk, he held the castle, town, and manor of Eye, the manors of Haughley and Thorndon, the hundreds of Hartismere and Stow, the manors of Syleham, Fressingfield, Huntingfield, Stradbrooke, Swarmes,, Hurtes, Mandevilles, Benhale, Bokling, Cantalee juxta Snape, Weyses manor in Stratford, Walsham, Westlefield, Cotton, Frestenden, Dagworth, Creeting St. Olave, the manor and hundred of Mutford, the manors of Kedding and Kettlebaston, the hundred of Lothingland, and the castle and manor of Wingfield. Besides this large enumeration, he possessed manors and castles in various other counties, with chests of gold, and heaps of valuables in silver and precious stones.

In the twenty-sixth year of the reign of Henry the Sixth, the date of William De la Pole assuming the Dukedom of Suffolk, the king granted his favorite forty pounds per annum, out of the Fee Farm of the town of Ipswich. Dugdale says that this advancement was imputed to have been made to him for advising the murder of the Duke of Gloster.* If this be the true interpretation of his advancement to the dignity, it clearly proves that the death of Gloster was approved, if not planned, by Henry himself.

We find from entries made about this period in the great court book of the corporation, that a celebrated Guild, called Corpus Christi, existed in the town. It also appears that a pageant was connected with

* Dugdale's Baronage.

it, to which the greatest attention was paid, not
only by the commonalty, but also by the municipal
authorities of the place. Nor was the patronage of
the corporation confined to their mere sanction or
protection given to the establishment, for it is
found that the funds of the town were, when
required, employed to add to the glory of the
exhibition which took place on certain days in
honour of the Guild. An officiating priest was
appointed, to whom certain mill profits were given
in payment of holy rites to be performed in honour
of "Corpus Christi"—this being the name given
to the institution. Indeed the funds of the town
were, it would seem, at all times to be commanded
in order to advance the appearance of the Guild.
The entries are too curious, and too closely illustra-
tive of the era and the particular circumstance to
which they refer, to be lost sight of. They shew
that were the Corporation tried by the spirit which
actuates modern courts of justice, every member
thereof would have stood a most perilous chance of
being amerced in a conviction of bribery and corruption.

Thursday after Allsaints—23 Henry 6th—1444.

John Causton, admitted and sworn Free-burgess,
upon condition that for seven years next following,
he shall maintain the Ornaments belonging to Corpus
Christi Pageant and the Stages, receiving the
charges thereof from the Farmers of the Common
Marshe, and the Portmans' Meadow, as the Bayliffs
for the time being shall think meet.

*St. Mark's Day—24th Henry 6th—*1445.

An Alderman of the Guild elected, and to him is granted to have the profits of the marchandize of Stones.

*Friday after Holy-rood—Edward 4th—*1479.

John Squer, Clerk, shall have the profits of the Mill-stones during his life, to be a Chaplain to celebrate Holy Rights in honour of Corpus Christi, and shall give security the same to do, and the residue of the profits shall go to the use of the Town of Ipswich.

If any Burgess shall refuse to pay 16d. yearly to Corpus Christi, he shall forfeit his Burgess-ship, and if any one shall bring with him to dinner more than his wife, he shall pay for every such person 4d.

The Guild Chaplain shall celebrate 30 days mass for every brother or sister of the Guild which shall die in the Town, which shall be done in the same Church of the Parish where he or she died.

Every Burgess inhabitant shall pay to the Master of the Grammar School 3d. per 2 weeks and no more, and the Master of the same School shall, during his life, celebrate for the Guild of Corpus Christi.

*Monday after Rogation—6th Henry 7th—*1490.

The Earl of Oxenford made Free-burgess of this Town, and one of the Brethren of the Guild.

The Prior of Ely is made Free-burgess, and of the Fraternity of the Guild.

Monday in Whitsun Week—6th Henry 8th.

All the utensils belonging to Corpus Christi Guild shall be entered in a Book, to be kept safe by John Butler, for the use of the Guild, viz. :—

1 Dozen of Spoons, 11½ oz.	5 Table Cloths
5 Mazers, 44½ oz.	3 Cloths of ¾-cloth
1 Pair	A Garnish of Vessells
14 Salts	2 Chargers
2 Brass Potts	5 Platters
4 Dishes	5 Saucers

The Friday in the 2nd week in Lent—
32nd Henry 8th—1540.

All the Burgesses shall bring the Sacrament of Corpus Christi from Lawrence Church towards the Fish Market to the Corn Hill, and so to the Tower Church, and so from thence on Corpus Christi day to Margaret's Green, and then round about the Towne to the Tower Church againe, and then shall hear a Mass; and on the next day shall bring the same from thence through Brook Street into the Fish Market and Corn Hill, and so to Lawrence Church, and here to end.

And that every of the Portmen shall have two Torches, and every of the 24 one Torch, and all the Torches shall wait on the Sacrament upon all the said three days, under forfeiture of 12d. for every default, and each Portman shall upon the same penalty wait upon the Sacrament upon the Sunday.

19th of Decembir—25th Elizabeth—1582.

The School master shall have 40 Shillings for his pains and charges, in presenting cirtain Pageants in joy of the Queen's Coronation upon the last 17th day of Novembir.

And it is agreed, that John Kinge, who lately made shew of a certain Pageant in form of a Shippe, with certain convenient speeches theron, at the last Guild holden within the Towne, at his owne charges, shall be allowed towards his said charges in that behalf, on and besides such money as he hath received already of the Alderman of the Guild, 5 marks to be paid out of the Tresury.

It has been considered, by some of the most learned bibliopoles, that Bishop Bale's play of "King Johan" was written by its author for the purposes of the Ipswich Guild, and performed upon the day of its anniversary. The existence of this curious dramatic performance has been made more apparent to the public by its publication in the works of the Camden Society, an association of antiquaries, and lovers of old English literature, who have combined for the praiseworthy object of perpetuating and rendering accessible whatever is valuable, but at the same time little known, among the materials for the civil, ecclesiastical, or literary history of the united kingdom. The MSS. from which the edition has been printed belongs to the collection of the Duke of Devonshire, and originally formed a part of a heap of papers belonging to the ancient corporation of Ipswich. Mr. J. P. Collier, the author of the History of English Dramatic Poetry, states that its existence was only incidentally known when that work was published, and in a preface to the drama says, that the composition was possibly written for the municipal authorities, and that it might reasonably be conjectured that it was performed by the Guild or trades of the town, in the same manner as similar plays were enacted at Chester, York, Coventry, and other places. Another circumstance, strengthening the probability of Bale having written it for the purpose of the Ipswich Corpus Christi, is the fact that Bale was a native of the county, and mentions Ipswich in his production. Thus speaking personally of king John he says:—

" Great monymentes are in Jppeswych, Donwych, and Berye,
  Which noteth him to be a man of netable mercye."

The date when the play was written is uncertain; but although there are allusions in the conclusion to Elizabeth, it is thought they are but additions, and that the drama was originally composed and acted before 1552—the date when Bale was made Bishop of Ossory.

The Guild, for which this curious drama was composed, was one of many to be found established in the towns of Suffolk. Their institution was avowedly—a confederation for general benefit in trade, but they were often created for the purpose of aiding charity and religion. Most of them derived their power from the crown, and were licensed by it. By these licenses they held equal benefits with those of monasteries, as they could become owners of lands, could erect chapels and altars for their own purposes, administer oaths, and as we have seen, with reference to Ipswich Corpus Christi Guild, appoint and pay their own priest, under authority, and out of local funds. It is considered that the institution resembled, in many respects, the modern benefit societies, and that the annual meeting of the latter, with the parade they exhibit through the streets in some places, is the remnant of the more imposing processions on the anniversary of the former.

The origin of Guilds is of remote antiquity. They are mentioned in Doomsday Book; and there is an instance of a Guild existing in Abbotsbury, in Dorsetshire, as early as the days of Canute. The Guild at Bury was established previously to 1182— the Merchants' Guild at Yarmouth, in 1207—but the time of their greatest increase was in the fifteenth and sixteenth centuries, or 1400 and 1500. John was a great friend to these fraternities, which affords us another presumption that the play of " King Johan" was written for Corpus Christi.

These confederations were suppressed by an act passed in the latter part of the reign of Henry the Eighth, and although a promise was made that their property should be appropriated to the same purposes as the Guilds enjoined, yet to a great extent the performance was nugatory; and as much of each particular fund was given away in the support of decayed or impoverished members of trading communities, its withdrawal was the cause of deep and

extensive distress throughout the poorer classes.
With respect to the Corpus Christi Guild at Ipswich, it appears that the act of suppression did not
affect it, as the last entry in the court books which
we have quoted is dated in the twenty-fifth of Elizabeth, 1582. The time when the Guild ceased is,
we believe, unknown.

It appears that the Grammar School existing in the
town is an establishment of very ancient date, as it
is found in 1477. At a Great Court of the corporation, it was ordered "that the master should have
the government of all scholars within the liberties
of the town." We have already seen that the
master of this school was appointed to act as chaplain of the Guild, in order that his means of suste-
nance should be increased. The value of this post
was, however, considerably enhanced in 1482, by a
person named Richard Felaw, a portman of the
town, leaving lands, in Whitton, and a house, for
this purpose. The Grammar School, however,
afterwards merged in the College erected by Cardinal Wolsey. Upon the fall of that establishment,
and the disgrace of the founder, the charter was
renewed by Henry the Eighth, and confirmed by
Elizabeth.

During the reigns of Henry the Eighth and his
daughter Mary, Ipswich became the scene of several
burnings and sacrifices, for the rights of conscience.
In 1555, the second year of Mary, mention is made
that the minister of East Bergholt, Robert Samuel,
was detected in being married, and after being

tracked to Ipswich, where his wife resided, he was
taken into custody by the order of a man named
Foster, living at Copdock, and conveyed to Norwich.
Here the offender against the laws of the Catholic
priesthood was thrown into gaol, and loaded with
chains. This punishment having no effect upon
his spirit, he was removed to this town, where he
was publicly and inhumanly burnt at the stake, in
the year 1555.

Indeed, as Fox the Martyrologist informs us,
much persecution existed in Ipswich, not only
against those who were adherents of the reformed
religion, but in earlier times, before protestantism
had taken root in the land. The following list of
persons proscribed on account of their faith, exists
on a broadside preserved in the library of the
Mechanics' Institution. It shows that a pretty
close eye was accustomed to be kept on those who
believed not the doctrines of the state, and that
there were, among the inhabitants of Ipswich in
the time of Queen Mary, those who were disposed
to run all risks, even to the forsaking of their homes
and hearths, for the sake of that freedom of conscience which fortunately we, of the present day,
have the power and the happiness to possess.

"A complaint against such as favoured the gospell
in Ipswich, exhibited to Queene Marie's Counsaile,
sittyng in commission at Beckles in Suffolke, the
18 of May, Ann. 1556, by Phillip Williams, alias
Footeman, John Steward, and Mathew Butler,
sworne for the purpose.

F

The names of such as fled out of the Towne and lurked in secret places.

S. Mary Tower.

Robert Partriche.

Rose Nottingham, daughter of William Nottingham the elder.

S. Laurence.

Anne Fenne, servaunt to Robert Nottingham.

Andrewe Ungforbye his wife and daughter.

Thomas Thompson, shomaker, supposed to have resceived but twise these 17 years.

Marten Algate, lockesmith, his wife.

S. Margaret's.

William Pickesse, tanner.

John Whoodles, couerlet weauer, and his wife.

William Darset, bricklaier.

Thomas Fowler, shomaker.

W. Wright his wife, at the windmill.

Laurence Waterwarde late curate, borne in a towne called Chorley in Lankeshire.

S. Clement's, Anno. 1558.

Mistresse Tooley, who departed to Darsham in Suff.

Agnes Wardal, the elder widowe.

Robert Wardal, her sonne.

S. Mathewe's.

John Shoomaker and his wife.

The names of such as have not receiued the Sacrament.

S. Clemente's.

Robert Bray.

John Nottingham.

Agnes Wardal, wife of Robert Wardal.

Nicholas Nottingham.

Richard Mitchel.

William Jordane, his wife.

Richard Butteral.

Robert Browne.

S. Peter's.

John Reade.

Thomas Spurdance.

John, Seruaunt to Stephen Grinleffe.

S. Stephen's.

Robert Scolding.

S. Margaret's.

John Greenewich and his wife.

S. Nicholas.

Thomas Sturgeon, mariner.

John Finne his wife.

S. Mary Keye.

Robert Branstone, seruaunte and brother to William Branstone.

S. Mary Tower.

Marten Johnson who lieth bed rede, Agnes Bent, his keeper, seruauntes to Rob. Nottingham.

S. Laurence.

Robert Sylke his son.

S. Mary at Elmes.

John Ramsey and his wife, now in prisone.

Names of such as obserued not ceremonies.
S. Clement's.
Robert Cambridge

Robert Brage his wife refused to suffer anye childe to be dipped in the font.

Joane Barber, widow, and Thomasine her daughter refused to behold the elevation of the sacrament.

Mistress Ponder, mother to Joane Barber, in the same fault.

Tie, a mariner his wife.
S. Mary at Elme's.
Richard Dawarde refused the   at masse in S. Laurence.

M. Lyons at masse at St. Mary Stoke refused the
S. Nicholas.
Widow Swaine.

Mathew Birde and his wife.

Stephen Greenwich and his wife.

Wil Colman, seruant to the sayde Stephen.

Robert Colman, and his wife.

Roger Laurence, *alias* Sparowe.

John Carelton, sadler.

William Colman.

James Dearst.
S. Peter's.
Richard Douce, apprentise with Nicholas Nottingham.

Rich. Bedley, a seller of hereticall bookes.
S. Stephen's.
James Bockyng, shoomaker, his wife.

John Rawe, late servaunt to James Ashley.

William Palmer, Rich. Richman, John Deearsley, seruaunts to Steuen Grene, shoomaker.

Rich. Richman, shoomaker, his wife, daughter to Mother Fenkell, midwyfe.

S. Peter's.

Mother Fenkell and Joan Warde *alias* Bentleys wife refuse to haue childerenne dipped in fontes.

S. Stephen's.

Mother Beriffe, midwife, refuseth to haue childre dipped in fontes.

S. Nicholas.

George Bushe, his wife resisted the hoast after receit of it.

Names of Priestes wiues that have accesse to their husbandes.

Rafe Carleton his wife, curate of S. Mathewe's and S. Mary at Elmes.

Elizabeth Cantiel wife to Rafe Cantiel

Jane Barker wife to Robert Barker, prieste, late of Burie.

Latimer his wife, curate of S. Laurence and S. Stephen's.

William Clearke his wife, late curate of Barkcham, and S. Mary at Elmes.

Names of mainteiners against this complaint.

Robert Sterop, customer to Nucene Maric.

Gilbert Sterop, deputie to Edwarde Brunstone, Esquier, for his butlerage.

Mister Butter the elder searcher.

Maistresse Tooly, swellynge by muche ritchesse into wealth.

Margaret Bray, who also presumeth uppon the office of a midwife not called.

S. Clement's.

Joane Barber, widowe, Mistresse Birde, practising muche wholesome counsell.

S. Mary Keye.

Bastian Mannes, wife, and himself more riche then wise.

Their requests to punish and conuent certaine, whose ensample might reuerse others from their opinions, as—

To conuent Richard Bird, gailer, who by euill counsel doth animate his prisoners of his secte, also for that he with his wife did checke us openly with unseemely woordes, tending almost to a tumult.

To couente Thomas Sadler, for certaine woordes spoken to John Bate the crier of the towne, the sixte of Maye.

That it might please the Bishop to wish his commissarie and official to be upright and diligente in theyr office, and appoynt a curate of more abilitie to feede his cure with God's woorde.

That none may be suffered to be midwiues but such as are catholicke, because of euill counsel at such times as the necessitie of womennes trauaile shall require a number of woman assembled.

That Rafe Carleton, curate, may be conuented

whether by corruption of money he hath ingrossed
his boke, of any that are there named, and hathe not
receyued in deede as it is reported."

This document has never before been published.
One further instance of persecution, and we have
done with this part of the subject.

In a chapel dedicated to St. George, standing
within the parish of St. Matthew's, and near the
site of the present church, Bilney, a protestant, was
accustomed to preach; and becoming offensive, he
was at length pulled from his pulpit, and led to
London to be examined by the proper authorities
touching his heresies. One of his examiners was
Cardinal Wolsey, who did not distinguish himself
for using moderation upon the occasion. It appears
to be somewhat uncertain if Bilney suffered at
Ipswich, Cambridge, or London. Burned at the
stake, he was somewhere, however, and added the
sacrifice of his life to the list of those who died in
the same cause of protestation against the church of
Rome.

At length the happy time arrived when persecution ceased. The cry of the people had gone forth
against all such abominations, and the arm of destruction fell on those who had aided and abetted
either iniquity or cruelty. The ancient mummeries
which had disgraced popery, at length by their
enormity opened the eyes of the people, and a sad
retributive justice was at hand. At the period of
which we now speak, there existed in Lady-lane,
St. Matthew's, a chapel, in which was kept an

image of "Our Lady," considered by the weak to be endowed with the power of working miracles of the most astounding nature. This was now removed in obedience to an order from London to that effect. It was taken, we believe, to Smithfield, and there, in the presence of a large assembly, burned to ashes.

No doubt exists that the properties of the church of Rome in the town were of considerable notice, and that much of them fell into the hands of those who considered they had a right to them. Many years since—though still within the term of modern date—a discovery was made in the church chest of St. Lawrence, fully proving this fact. Among a quantity of ancient papers was found a receipt given by the King's Commissioners for the sale of church property, for money arising from eight copes of gold, 487 ounces of silver plate, and vestments covered with gold lace. This document was dated in the last year of the reign of Edward the Sixth, namely, 1553.

Having brought our narrative down to the period of the Reformation, we here leave that portion which may be denominated the ancient history of Ipswich. We shall, therefore, endeavour to give the particulars of its modern history, from the era when Elizabeth ascended the throne of these realms down to the present period.

MODERN HISTORY OF IPSWICH.

On the 10th day of June, 1561, Queen Elizabeth ordered that all the inhabitants of Ipswich should be taxed—or rather assessed in payment of the expenses of Her Majesty's visit to the town. It was also determined upon—so decided were the Councils of the maiden Queen, to leave no doubt whatever that the debts incurred in Her Majesty's entertainment should be liquidated, that such individuals as did not pay due attention to the order of assessment, should stand disfranchised from that time forth, and never more be capable of receiving, for the benefit of themselves or families, those immunities which the Queen had bestowed on the town by the confirmation of all its charters by inspeximus on the 23rd day of September, in the year previous to the publication of the fiscal order. There were a few defaulters to the fund for the honourable reception of the Queen, though not so great in number as to prevent a sufficient collection to aid the royal visit. To this town the royal lady came twice, and no doubt the reception given, proved sufficiently to her royal mind that the inhabitants were as devoted to the new order of things as the most zealous friends of protestantism could well desire.

It would appear however that the careful administration of the rites of religion, owing perhaps to that negligence, which—happily, generally but short-lived—follows in the wake of all great changes, was but as yet ill conducted. We find that the Queen expressed herself much dissatisfied with the " lack of gowns worn by the clergy." It was considered also that the bishop of the diocese was but remiss in attention to his onerous and priestly duties, inasmuch as reports, to a certain extent uncontradicted, had gone abroad, that he not only was lax in detecting schismatics, but actually winked at their doings when he found them. Complaint was also made—for as yet the whole of the unnatural customs of the papistry had not been extirpated—that there existed too many clergymen's wives, children and orphans, living about in cathedral towns and such colleges as had been spared from the general wreck of monachism. To remedy these evils, a remonstrance was made to the bishop, as to his proportion of the general blame, and Her Majesty issued an order from this town, declaring that such ecclesiastics as should harbour women in their cathedrals or colleges, should lose their promotions. Her Majesty also, for the better keeping of the churches, and for the better maintenance of the ministers, caused an act to be passed for the augmentation of the value of their benefices, under which law a sum of money was ordered to be raised,

to the amount thought necessary, once in every
year. This obligation on the inhabitants of the
several parishes applying, is now levied by order of
the town council, such parish first showing clearly
that the money is needed for the purpose.

At the passing of the Municipal Reform Bill, it
was conjectured that as the application must be
made in open court, and the parish officers compelled to prove the strict necessity of the application, that the infusion of a dissenting party into the
corporation would have the effect of causing
the rejection of such application. Such anticipa-
tion has, however, been proved erroneous in its
result. Every application of the kind has been
received and granted, where the right to such aid
has been deemed unquestionable and the necessity
evident.

To particularize at any length the numerous acts
which passed the legislature, or even to give a
summary of the regulations made by the local
authority to improve the town, and to increase
commerce, would only be to enter on subjects likely
to tire by their number, prolixity, and minuteness
of detail. Some mention must, however, be made
of those matters as give us a clear and broad view
of the progress made towards that order of things
which, happily for us, obtains in the present day.

In the early years of the reign of Elizabeth, an
order was published for the better order of the
Grammar School, in strict conformity with the
charter of the establishment. The first notice of an

exhibition from this school exists in the sum of
fifty-three shillings and fourpence being paid to a
poor, but "toward young man, named Robert
English." A proper salary for the master usher of
the school was also settled on the 18th of March,
1565.

In 1570—being the thirteenth year of the reign
of Elizabeth—the first act for paving the town was
passed, which has since been superseded by others
of a more modern date, embodying those improvements and extensions which the growth of the
town peremptorily required.

In the thirty-eighth year of Elizabeth, it was
ordered that the port of Ipswich should fit out two
ships for the general defence of the nation, and
accordingly two vessels were provided, severally
termed the Katherine, burthen 123 tons, and the
William, 140 tons, with a crew of thirty men. A
few years previous to this date, we find the comparative strength of the Suffolk ports in commercial
shipping stated, which will show the amount of trade
carried on at the port. The port of Aldborough
owned fifty-four ships, most or all mere coasters,
manned by 120 men. The neighbouring port of
Woodbridge only owned six vessels, their crew
amounting to eighteen sailors. Southwold owned
twenty ships, with 100 men; and Ipswich, though
possessed of but few vessels, yet employed 190 men.
The document from whence this account is taken is
preserved in the Cottonian Library, and states the
number of vessels belonging to the town and port

of Ipswich to be but six. This, however, must be
an error, for as the number of men employed is
stated at 190, it would give an average of more than
thirty men to each vessel, and tend to prove that
vessels of heavier tonnage were accustomed to visit
the port at that period, and that the channel of the
Orwell was much deeper than at present. However,
in the next year of this reign, 1596, it is found that
two Ipswich vessels, namely the Corslet, carrying,
soldiers and sailors together, 140 men, and the
James, with 144 men, were present at the expedition to Cadiz.

In the third year of the reign of James the
Second, all the charters granted by previous sove-
reigns were confirmed, and the town made progress
in population and increase of buildings until the
days of Charles the First and Second. In 1654,
however, a great fire took place in the town, which
accident was productive of great damage; and in
1660, in order to assist in refilling the coffers of
Charles the Second, it was voted that £300 be paid
out of the town treasury, besides a sum raised by
voluntary subscription.

In the year 1604, the plague raged in the town to
a considerable extent, as the following extracts from
the Court Book of the corporation will abundantly
show.

"At a Great Court held at Ipswich, 14*th July*,
1603—1*st James* 1*st*—

It is agreed, that the Waggenors that com from
London, shall not be suffered to come into the

Towne, before they have certified unto the Bailiffes upon their Othes, what persons and things they bring therein, and that such things as are suspicious, shall be utterly forbidden, and likewise that the Hoye-men that shall come from London, with having no passengers, shall come no nearer to Towne than Dunham Bridge before they made certificate unto the Bailiffs that they bring no sickness that is infectious into the Towne.

25th July, 1603—1st James 1st.

It is agreed that Mr. Carnebie, Mr. Lowe, Mr. Ward, and Mr. Parkhurste, shall enquire, and find out of the Towne 4 of the fittest men to attend uppon the infected houses and people, if any shall be for the buriall of them, and for the deliverie of meate and drink for them, and 2 women for the leyinge of them forthe, and viewing of them and attending to them in their sickness. And that as well the men and women as the infected shall be kept at the comon chardge, and that a collection shall be made of evrie inhabitant chardged in the Subsidie Booke, towards the said chardge of the said people, and ev'rie man taxed for land shall paie thereunto 3d. of the pound, and ev'rie one taxed for goods, shall paie after the rate of 2d. in the pounde, and that others that are not in the Subsidie Books, shall be rated by the discretion of the Bailiffs, and the Collectors of the said taxation to be appointed by Mr. Bailiffs.

26th July, 1603—*1st James 1st.*

It is agreed, John Cole and Wm. Forsdyke shall be employed about the buriall of suche persons as are dead, or shall die within the Towne, and shall have 16d. a-day for every day as long as the Bailiffs shall think mete, and they shall remaine in the house builded for them, and they shall have such victualls and things brought them, and such daylie wages as they shall require, which such persons shall go abroad in the Towne, when occasion shall serve, about the said business, with white wands or rodds in their hands, so as to be known from other men. And it is agreed, that the persons that shall die, shall be wound uppe in course Soutage, and that Anne Spalding shall have 3s. allowed her weeklie, and meate and drincke for her attendance upon Garrod and his wife and children, and suche others as shall be sicke of the infection during the time she may be employed, and that John Kirke shall attend upon the said persons, and fetch them victuals and other necessaries, and shall be allowed 7s. a-week from this time.

18th September, 1603—*1st James 1st.*

It is agreed, that noe Shippes, Hoyes, or Vessells whatsoever belonging to this Towne, shall be brought any nearer the Towne than Greenwiche Nesse, and if any of owners or masters of the said shippes, or other vessels, or anie of them shall offende contrarie to this order, that then he or they, soe offendinge therin, shall be imprisoned during Mr. Bailiffs pleasure.

And it is agreed, that there shall be warding ev'rie daie in the weeke, at the places hereafter named   att Stoke Bridge, att Handford Bridges, att Mr. Durrell's House, and att Stoning Crosse, by two sufficient householders at ev'rie of the said places, who shall examine such men as are suspicious, or to be suspected, for bringinge the sicknesse into this Towne, and if any suspicious person shall com or bringe goods into the Towne, then they to signifie the same unto the Hedberrow, that shall be appoynted to overveiwe them to the extent that Mr. Bailiffs may be informed thereof.

11th January, 1604—1st James 1st.

It is agreed that Cole and Forsdyke shall have paid them for the burial of such as shall die of the Infection, within the said Towne and liberties thereof, 3s. 6d. a-piece weeklie for the burial, and carrying them to buriall, and 6d. for the buriall of one that shall die of the infection beinge poore, and that Cole's wife shall have paid her 12d. a-week for serchinge of them that shall die of the infection, which monye shall be paid to the Chamblins of the Towne, during the Townes pleasure.

23rd January, 1604—1st James 1st.

It is agreed, that the weeklie payment to Cole his wife, and Forsdyke for the buriale and serchinge of the infected persons, shall contynue until Thursdaie come se'nnight, and if in the mean season that none shall happen to die of the infection within that time, that then the said payment shall cease."

Another visit of the plague took place in 1666, producing the greatest distress.

The burial place of those who died victims to these awful visitations, is believed to have been near the ancient church of St. Austin, on the Stoke side of the river. Great numbers of human bones have been found on this spot.

In 1678, Charles the Second, in order that no inconvenience might arise out of irregular elections of the officers of the town, granted a charter, in which express directions were made with regard to the filling up of vacancies. The execution and non-execution of the clauses and provisions of this charter have at various times, instead of removing difficulties, tended to increase them.

In 1678, another charter, confirmatory of others which had passed the royal seal of previous monarchs, was granted by Charles the Second. This document was obtained for the purpose of settling all disputes relative to the mode in which the authorities should be elected, and is said to be that by which the appointment of official persons has been regulated, from this period to the time when the remodelling of all municipal bodies took place under the Municipal Reform Bill. Though enacted, however, for this worthy purpose, it failed to produce an uniformly good effect, as it did not prevent the arising of much difficulty from the election of Bailiffs, Portmen, and others. This charter was, in consequence of distractions and the affairs of the corporation getting into a very melan-

choly condition, surrendered to the crown at the
latter part of the reign of Charles the Second,
accompanied by a petition for a new charter, which
act of royal condescension—for such it was termed
—was received in Ipswich on the twenty-eighth of
July, 1685.

This newly conferred power, however, was not
suffered to remain long unmolested. It appeared
not to have been enrolled, consequently was of an
informal nature, and contained no legal force. At
the period, therefore, of the revolution of 1688, this
charter was annulled by James the Second, and a
restoration made of the old charter which had
preceded it.

In 1693, the manufacture of lutestring was
introduced into this town extensively. The corporation entered into an engagement with fifty families
of French protestants, that they should be located
within the walls, receive a donation of twenty
shillings each—that they should be excused from
rates, or serving any office for seven years—that a
church should be erected for their accommodation ·
free of expense, and that an allowance should be
made of twenty pounds per annum towards the
support of their minister. For a short period it
would appear that the manufacture of lutestring
flourished here; but it soon became absorbed into
Norwich, forming a component portion of the
settled manufactures of that industrious city.

Although it will at once be seen that out of the
tangled web of distraction and decay, in more than

a solitary instance, the "woof" of industry, prosperity and knowledge, was exhibiting itself, yet the fabric came from the loom of time, mixed occasionally with those darker threads to be found only in the product composing the earlier ages. Among other deep shadows resting on the face of society was the belief in witchcraft; and many individuals in the county, peculiar in their temperament, or behaviour, were sacrificed to cruelty and superstition. In the year 1645, it appears that the town of Ipswich was the residence of a notorious witch, who practised her sorceries on the unsuspecting or unwary. This beldame rejoiced in the name of Mother Lakeland, and was in process of time duly arraigned and condemned as a dealer in enchantments. Ultimately, however, she made a confession of her sins and iniquities before she departed this life, and in an old tract, entitled, " The Laws against Witches and Conjurations," the following relation of her believed iniquity is to be found.

" The Confession of Mother Lakeland, of Ipswich, · who was arraigned and condemned for a Witch, and suffered death by burning, at Ipswich, in Suffolk, on Tuesday, the 9th of September, 1645.

" The said Mother *Lakeland*, hath been a Professour of Religion, a constant hearer of the Word for these many years, and yet a *Witch* (as she confessed) for the space of near twenty years. The *Devil* came to her first between sleeping and waking, and spake to her in a hollow voyce telling her, that if she would serve him she should want nothing.

After often solicitation, she consented to him; then he stroke his claw (as she confessed) into her hand, and with her blood wrote the covenants. (*Now the subtility of Sathan is to be observed, in that he did not presse her to deny God and Christ, as he useth to do to others: because she was a Professour, and might have lost all his hold by pressing her too far.*) Then he furnished her with three Imps, two little Dogs, and a Mole (as she confessed), which she imployed in her services. Her husband she bewitched (as she confessed), whereby he lay in great misery for a time, and at last dyed. Then she sent one of her Dogs to *Mr. Lawrence*, in *Ipswich*, to torment him and take away his life: she sent one of them also to his Child, to torment it, and take away the life of it, which was done upon them both: and all this (as she confessed) was, because he asked her for 12s. that she owed him, and for no other cause.

"She further confessed, that she sent her Mole to a Maid of one *Mrs. Jennings*, in *Ipswich*, to torment her, and take away her life, which was done accordingly: and this for no other cause, but for that the said Maid would not lend her a needle that she desired to borrow of her, and was earnest with her for a shilling she owed the said Maid.

"Then she further confessed, she sent one of her Imps to one *Mr. Beale*, in *Ipswich*, who had formerly been a Suitor to her Grandchild; and because he would not have her, she sent and burned a new ship (that had never been at sea) that

he was to go Master of; and sent also to torment
him and take away his life; but he is yet living, but
in very great misery, and as it is verily conceived
by the Doctors and Chirurgeons that have him in
hand, that he consumes and rots, and that half of
his body is rotten upon him as he is living.

" Severall other things she did, for all which she
was by Law condemned to die, and in particular to
be burned to death, because she was the death of
her husband (as she confessed); which death she
suffered accordingly.

" But since her death, there is one thing that is
very remarkable, and to be taken notice of: That
upon the very day that she was burned, a bunch of
flesh, something after the form of a Dog, that grew
upon the thigh of the said *Mr. Beale*, ever since
the time that she first sent her Imp to him, being
very hard, but could never be made to break by all
the means that could be used, brake of itself, without any means using: And another sore, that at the
same time she sent her Imp to him, rose upon the
side of his belly, in the form of a Fistula, which
ran and could not be braked for all the means that
could be used, presently also began to heale, and
and there is great hopes that he will suddenly
recover again, for his sores heale apace, and he doth
recover his strength. He was in this misery for
the space of a yeare and a halfe, and was forced to
go with his head and his knees together, his misery
was so great."

We believe this is the last Ipswich sorceress,

whose confession is extant, though it is painful to
remark, that in various parts of this county the
ignorant practice of swimming harmless persons,
under the pretence of deciding whether they were
possessed or not, continued down to a much later
period.

From the time of which we are now speaking to
the year 1704, the inhabitants of the town had not
followed the example of quarrellings and bickerings
set them by the corporate authorities.   All was
peaceable with the great bulk of the commonalty;
and it is found that in the December of that year,
it was first mooted and decided, that a nightly
watch should be established, and that every person
called on to take the part of watchman, and refusing,
should forfeit a sum of money for such refusal.

In 1709, it would appear that the town had
suffered many reverses in trade and commerce ; as,
in answer to a communication made to the corporation to admit and employ certain German protestants, it was stated that by " reason of decay of
trade, and having no manufactory to employ poor
people, and the great burden and increase of its own
poor inhabitants," they could not possibly be
accommodated by the town.

In 1785, the disputes and intricacies of the corporation continuing, a committee was appointed to
make a report of the property and revenue of that
body, when it was found that although possessed of
a good estate, the debts and mortgages were so
heavy as to leave only £132. per annum unappro-
priated, for the current expenses.

In 1793, another act of Parliament was obtained
for paving the town, though strennously opposed, as
the measure was thought to encroach on the privileges of the corporation; yet it passed into a law,
and the first portion of the new pavement was laid
on the Cornhill, near the spot now occupied by the
Bell public-house.

In the next year, 1794, the Rotunda, a building
formerly standing on the Cornhill, was erected. It
was built on the site of the ancient Shambles, which
tradition stated to be the gift of Cardinel Wolsey's
father to the town, though this story, as far as
research will lead us, has no foundation in fact.

It was about this date that the river Gipping was
made navigable from this town to Stowmarket,
conferring on the general community of both
places, and the neighbouring country parts, a convenience which, though much desired, had not
hitherto been enjoyed. The navigation thus accomplished is sixteen miles in length, and the
stream employed to connect the two places runs
through a great variety of country, comprehending
some very fine views, as well as those close and
flat prospects connected with the features of this
district of England. The result of the work has
been a vast increase in the quantity of grain brought
from the internal parts of Suffolk for shipment at
the port of Ipswich, and the return of coal to the
interior. At the same period Handford Bridge was
erected, a work of no trifling nature, as the continu-
ation of the structure was obliged to be carried a

considerable distance across the head of the marshes. Previous to the erection of the bridge, it was no unusual occurrence for carriages to meet with accidents at this point, in consequence of the violence of the stream, and even at the present day, during the winter season, a thaw produces floods of such magnitude as materially to injure the arches of the marsh bridge. This was the case during the winter of 1840, when the structure sustained considerable injury by the rapid passage of water overflowing the banks of the Gipping. The total expense of the construction of the Stowmarket navigation was nearly £27,000.

This small stream, the Gipping, gave an early name to Ipswich, in the cognomen "Gippeswiche," which it some time bore. It takes its rise from three distinct points—the first near a village bearing the name of the stream, Gipping, a second at Rattlesden, and the third at Wetherden. These heads unite at Stowmarket.

In the same year, 1794, the borough determining to strengthen the hands of the government, then placing the whole kingdom in a state of defence against the anticipated invasion by the French insurgents, patronised the establishment of a body of military to be called the Ipswich Volunteers. This regiment was to be "virtually" raised by a reduced military officer named Robinson, and an address was forwarded to the Commander-in-chief for permission to establish the corps under him. The plan however was not carried into effect, though a band of men was afterwards organized, called the Loyal Ipswich Volunteers, over which the late Colonel Neale was at one period of their existence placed in command. This body numbered two hundred, and was bound, if required, to march to the relief of any part of the kingdom in case of actual invasion. The local militia regiment raised in the eastern portion of the county, and known by the name of the East Suffolk Militia, mustered stronger than any other similar body in the kingdom, and contained in its ranks some of the most wealthy individuals resident in the county. Indeed throughout the whole of the fearfully excited period of the French Revolution, the loyalty of Suffolk stood pre-eminent, and many instances are on record of self-devotion and extreme liberality to the cause.

The close neighbourhood of Ipswich with the coast, and the proximity of that coast with Holland and the more northern states, rendered it exceedingly eligible as a garrison town during the long and bloody wars which Great Britain waged on the continent of Europe. .Under this circumstance, the town at these periods was generally filled with soldiers, and partook more of the appearance of the depot of arms in a country under military occupation, than a peaceful commercial port. Barracks were erected in various parts, namely, on the old dock side—the Woodbridge Road—and at the end of St. Matthew's Street. These buildings, with the exception of those in St. Matthew's parish, have been removed, or converted to other purposes.

The Barracks existing were built in 1795, and are calculated to accommodate three troops of horse—the regiment being divided between this place and Norwich. The head quarters of the regiment are most generally held here, though there have been a few instances in the last twenty years of their being located at Norwich. It has, however, been found by the officers of regiments, that independently of superior accommodation—agreeable and airy situation to be found in the Barracks at Ipswich—the good feeling and friendship which has always existed between the families of the neighbouring part of the county and the military, has been far more than a compensation for a location in a larger and more-bustling place. Through these circumstances Ipswich has always been a favourite spot of residence with soldiers.

At the close of the war, the town gradually lost its military character, and assumed that of a place intended by nature to become the seat of considerable commerce. The inhabitants increased, and with the increase of people, trade poured its wealth and comforts into all the channels of population. Old public buildings became improved—new ones erected, and since that period the town has progressed in improvement, wealth, and population, in a ratio unprecedented in this part of the empire. This will be seen in the enumeration and history of edifices erected for public purposes, and the comparison of the amount of population at various times, and the amount of trade in different years.

In order that the stranger might be well acquainted with the nature of the trade of Ipswich, we must premise that the county of Suffolk, of which she is the capital town, forms the most eastern portion of England, and from its peninsular form is separated from the great lines of traffic traversing the kingdom. Indeed it may almost be termed a country by itself, so entirely and distinctly is it divided from the main body of the nation. Its productions are chiefly agricultural, a small portion only of the skill of its inhabitants being engaged in manufactures, with the exception, which it may be necessary to state, of a fabric of linen called Suffolk hemp, and a portion of the silk weaving trade. Its surface is therefore laid out in multitudinous farms of grazing and corn land. Large quantities of barley are also grown, and when converted into malt, are shipped from Ipswich to various parts of the kingdom. The business of the port is not, however, confined to the granary trade, but includes a considerable commerce with other parts of the kingdom, in various descriptions of merchandize—the usual imports from foreign countries, and an export trade with the continent and other places.

To the traveller who had only become acquainted with the manufacturing districts of England, Suffolk would exhibit a total dissimilitude if he made a tour through her confines. He would cease to find the manufacturing village peopled by its two or three thousand weavers and spinners, at each step of his journey. No tall chimney rising upward and

almost reaching the clouds—and if not reaching so
great an altitude, still making an ebon atmosphere for
itself, is noticed scattered at intervals over the face
of the landscape, at once recording pillars, marking
the triumphs of mechanical skill, and monuments
erected to commemorate the death of agriculture.
All is sylvan and arcadian.   Wide tracts of heathy
ground where graze unnumbered flocks—extensive
ox pastures—farms entirely arable, the produce of
whose fertile fields, in the ripening time of autumn,
gleams like a golden covering thrown over them—
meet the eye on every side.   Indeed the breadth of
corn sown in Suffolk is considered by far the largest
grown by any county in the kingdom, and of course
forms a considerable item in the general supply
required for the subsistence of the whole country.

As Ipswich, and the county in which she stands,
possesses no mineral or manufacturing wealth, it is
plain that she must depend for existence upon the
amount of her exports and imports—her exports
being mainly the agricultural produce of Suffolk,
and her imports those of home product and the
manufacture of foreign countries.   Her greatness
must, therefore, altogether depend upon the good or
ill condition of agriculture and the prosperity of her
inhabitants.   Every event, every rise and fall in price
of natural production, every bad season, must inevitably, more or less, raise or depress her condition.
Still of the natural progression caused by the increase
in population—the Wet Dock—and let us add, in
hope, the Rail-road—nothing else than the establish-

ment of a rival port can deprive her. This is not to
be looked for, as the only port at all likely to compete
with her is kept down, in her energies to become
something better than she is at present, by the shallow waters, and other unconquerable obstacles of
her river. We allude to Woodbridge, and the river
Deben, which runs up to her quay. Harwich, on
the eastern-most coast of Essex, and at the very
point where the Orwell enters the land, has been
mentioned as likely to affect the prosperity of
Ipswich, were a rail-road carried from the eastern
counties' line to the former place, because Harwich
would then regain the continental packet station
which she has lost, inasmuch as the time of transition
would be swifter by rail-road from London to that
town, than it is to the same point by steam navigation from the Thames. Harwich has also a fine
and safe harbour, capable of accommodating a large
number of vessels, and therefore far better situated
than the port of Ipswich, only reached as it is by a
tortuous and difficult navigation. But with all
appliances and means of advantage, of which
Harwich by fortuitous circumstances may become
possessed, there exists not the remotest probability
that she will raise herself into the position of a
rival to Ipswich. It must be remembered that
Ipswich is a Suffolk port—exporting especially the
production of the soil of the county, and receiving
in return such commodities as are required in exchange. Harwich, in the event of being restored
to the dignity of a packet station, may draw to

herself the trade of some of the small Essex seaports, but even should she create merchants of her
own, and gather to herself more of modern speculation than as yet appertains to her, she will not then
draw towards her one single particle of the commerce of Ipswich. However great the prosperity
of the county of Suffolk, it must be exclusively
shared by this latter town, and no circumstance can
deprive her of its participation.

The completion of the eastern line of rail-road
will however prove of the greatest benefit to our
port. The closer and more frequent communication between men beget connections ending in
profit and advantage to all parties concerned. It
has been proved to demonstration, beyond the
power of doubt, that the advantages secured to the
town of Birmingham by the London and Birmingham Railway are immense, and when the powers of
the undertaking are fully and completely developed,
will be abundantly increased. There is not a town,
nor a station upon the course of that particular
line, not benefited by the rail. This is the case
in comparatively solitary places where, for the
convenience of distance, stations have been established by the company. Towns are likely to spring
up where mere villages had previously existed; and
where stood but a few cottages or a single house,
the spots are rapidly gathering into villages. What
then must be the effect of the passing of the eastern
counties' line through Ipswich but added prosperity,
and an increase in the number of its inhabitants.

In whatever light we survey the town or port of Ipswich, we cannot avoid being struck with her great improvement. She has now a rapid, constant, and highly improved communication with the metropolis and the coast of Essex by sea. The steam-boat has brought the port and all her dependencies within a seven hours' voyage of London. The river Orwell by the same means has been rendered open to all parties at all times. Not a ferry upon her banks exists, but can now be visited by the curious or the man of business every day. This fine and noble stream, with all its beauties and associations, is no longer what it has been, a comparatively closed book to all but the professed voyager to other parts, who took the course of the Orwell as part of his high road. It is a path well known to every-day travellers, men of pleasure, of leisure, and of business. Through the power of steam the river is now becoming extensively known, and as extensively appreciated. What the steam-boat has done for the Hudson, the steam-boat is doing for the Orwell. It is making its beauties familiar to the lover of the picturesque—and its waters a more easy communication with the outer world than would ever be attained without its aid. These advantages have only just developed themselves. Time will increase them a thousand-fold.

At the same moment also that the river has been opened to all kinds of profitable, and let us add pleasurable, enterprise, we are not idle at home. Witness the extent, capability, and advantages derived by the creation of the Wet Dock. Noble fleets of merchantmen can be safely accommodated in its wide area. Hundreds of vessels can here rest in perfect safety from storm and tempest, and daily floated out to sea without harm or inconvenience. It no longer exists as an objection, that except at high water the keels of all ships visiting the port are laid bare and dry, to the extreme detriment of their timbers, and the danger of injury to their cargoes. Vessels of the heaviest tonnage the Orwell can bring to the lock-gates, are here accommodated with berths as redolent of the briny element, for all practical purposes, as the depths of the open ocean itself.

In our opinion, the completion of a rail-road to Ipswich from the metropolis, joined with steam navigation in the Orwell, will effect not only wonders for its own prosperity, but also greatly facilitate the continental trade generally. The whole commerce of the northern portion of the continent lies open to Ipswich. By the assistance of steam-boats how rapid would be the transit between the shores of Suffolk, Belgium, Holland, and Russia. Immediately opposite our coast lie most of the principal mercantile towns of the two former countries, and as easily reached from our own port as from any other in the eastern counties. The interchange of commodities effected by rapid steam-boats from Ipswich, would then be further facilitated by the Eastern Counties' Railway, carrying our share of the exchange upon wings fleeter than the winds

into the heart and the remotest parts of the kingdom. This trade too must be exclusively connected with Ipswich, for what advantage would
Harwich derive in this case from her highly boasted
superior station? None. The utmost facility of
communication over this port is now, and would
still be but one hour—the time occupied in vessels
traversing the Orwell from Ipswich, to the point in
which Harwich stands, and her starting place upon
such voyages. Our port at the present moment has
a large and increasing trade, not only with the continental towns we have mentioned, but also with
other parts of the world. This trade be it recol-
lected is carried on without the assistance of a
single steamer, and in vessels not noted for swift
sailing. How much it must be increased, were
there but a well appointed line of steamers employed
in the traffic, it is not easy to conjecture.

If we add to the advantages already enumerated
the establishment of the Eastern Counties' Railway,
pouring into Ipswich, as it will do, a living tide
of strangers from distant parts, bent on all missions
to which the wants or desires of men can give rise,
we shall find that a concentration of advantages
has been created in our favour, and we may safely
hazard the prognostic, that in progress of time, when
all these various facilitators of civilization and commerce have given out the earnest of the strength
which is in them, that Ipswich will become, what
she is designed by her position to be, the Liverpool
of the east.

The principal church in the town is considered
to be ST. MARY AT THE TOWER, situated a few yards
in the rear of the left hand side of Tavern Street.
It is a perpetual curacy, the nomination being in
the hands of the parishioners. The present incumbent is the Rev. N. Leger. St. Mary at the
Tower, is a spacious and commodious building.
On the exterior of the porch is an ancient dial. In
the chancel stands a curious monument erected to
the memory of Mr. William Smart, a portman of
the town, who died in the year 1600. At the base
is painted a view of Ipswich. The inscription contains an acrostic on the name of the individual
whose memory it records. There is a fine brass
upon the pavement of the middle aisle, and against
the north wall stands a handsome monument,
representing a male and female figure kneeling with
an open book before them at an altar, attended by
two female and two male figures weeping. The
females bear each a skull in their laps. This
monument is erected to the memory of John
Robinson, a portman of Ipswich, who departed this
life in 1666, and Elizabeth his wife, who died in
1694. It also records the death of four of their
offspring.

The next building devoted to sacred purposes,
deserving notice for its architectural qualifications,
is the church of ST. MARGARET, erected near St.
Margaret's Green. Its exterior might perhaps be

considered too crowded in its details, but there are
many admirers of ecclesiastical architecture who do
not scruple to assert its equality with the best
churches of its size in the county. St. Margaret's
Church stands on or near the site of Trinity
Chapel, once attached to the priory of the Holy
Trinity. As late as the year 1674, a portion of
Trinity Church was standing, and either a part of
this building, or of the ancient priory, forms the
boundary line of the wall separating the churchyard
from the Park of Christ Church. The interior of
the church presents a curious · appearance, the
ceiling being singularly painted, and several ancient
carvings stand out from the walls. The exterior is
a strange mixture of styles, many of the important
members of which are very minutely treated. The
roof is of timber and well constructed. The church
also contains a curious font. The parliamentary
visitors when they came into Suffolk, removed from
St. Margaret's the twelve apostles in stone, and
desired that twenty or thirty pictures should be
taken away and destroyed.

The church of St. NICHOLAS stands in the lower
part of the town, not far from the Gipping. It is
supposed to have been erected upon the site of the
ancient church of St. Michael. St. Nicholas
Church was an impropriation to St. Peter's Priory,
which on the dissolution was granted to two individuals named Breton and Webb. It is a perpetual curacy only, and not of great value. The
exterior walls of the building show several pieces of

H 2

antiquity carved in stone, supposed to have belonged to the ancient priory. Within the church also some curious specimens of painting have been discovered behind a tomb. They represent—it is supposed—the Archangel St. Michael, to which Wolsey's father contributed by will the sum of forty shillings. During the progress of some repairs made in 1827, five urns or jars of a large size were found embedded in the wall of this church, but although evidently cinerial vessels, they did not appear to have at any time contained the dust or ashes of human bodies.

From the floor of this building, the parliamentary visitors took up three sepulchral brasses, and destroyed six religious pictures on the walls. Westward of the church, on the bank of the Gipping, stood a convent of Franciscan Friars. A small portion of this edifice long survived the general decay of the establishment.

St. Mary at the Key was impropriated to the Priory of St. Peter and Paul. The present building is very plain and simple, both internally and externally. The tower however is curiously built in flints, and is an object worthy of observation. The church spoliator, Dowsing, paid a visit to the edifice, and broke down nine superstitious pictures and destroyed many inscriptions.

A little beyond St. Mary Key Church stood, until within a few years, an ancient timber building, which, from its doors and windows being defended with wooden shutters, would almost

appear to have been built previously to the introduction of glass into household buildings. The
house of which we speak was a huge lumbering
edifice, formed almost entirely of wood, and stood
for many years unoccupied. It was, during the
year 1839, razed to the ground floor, and the
materials of which it was composed sold piecemeal
to the public.

St. Lawrence Church stands in St. Lawrence
lane. There are no particular features about the
present building, connecting it with architectural
beauty or antiquity. Old Weever tells us the original church was commenced by John Bottold in 1431.
He is buried within it. Here also reposes Edmund
Daundy, an individual who gave much of his sub-
stance in charity, and was a relative of Cardinal
Wolsey. He died in 1515. Behind the western
gallery of this church is a painting executed upon
the wall, of Christ disputing with the doctors. It
was painted by Sir R. K. Porter, when a young
man, during his sojourn in the garrison of this town.
A picture of Charles the First, lying in state,
formerly ornamented the altar, but within a few
years has been removed—being* considered most
probably a strange subject to occupy such a place.

St. Clement's Church, does not boast of great
antiquity. Its internal arrangements consist of two
aisles and a nave. In this church lies buried
Thomas Eldred, who accompanied Cavendish the
voyager round the world. The following inscription is upon his tomb:

" He that travels the world about,
   Seeth God's wonders, and God's works.

" Thomas Eldred travelled the world about and went out of Plimouth ye 2d July, 1586, and arrived in Plimouth again the 9th of September, 1588."

This church is generally used as the burial place of mariners dying in the town, and a number of tombs recording the decease of sailors are found in the building, and the adjoining churchyard.

St. Helen's Church appears to be a building of considerable antiquity, although the exact time of its erection is not ascertained by any authentic record. It has recently undergone considerable repair and enlargement.

The church of St. Mary at the Elms is, as its title imports, either dedicated to the Virgin, or to some female saint who contracted the odour of her sanctity upon the spot. To whomsoever dedicated, however, its origin dates of course from a catholic period, and the structure is supposed to have risen upon the ruins of a previous building of a sacerdotal character. The architecture is not of an imposing style, and the tower being built of brick, its peculiarly red colour renders the church strongly obtrusive on the eye. Appropriately with the title of the building, a fine row of elm trees stand in front. The neighbourhood of this church seems in early times to have been ornamented with many superior dwellings. Nearly opposite the churchyard is a more than commonly good specimen of a timbered house. An adjoining street, called Black

Horse lane, exhibits a residence with plastered
roses and panelling on its front; and in the rear of
the church itself are the remains of some ancient
erections evidently of high character. St. Mary
Elms is a perpetual curacy of small emolument.
The present incumbent is the Rev. W. Aldrich.

St. MATTHEW's CHURCH is situated at the west
entrance of the town, on the right hand side of St.
Matthew's street. The church is as unpretending
in its appearance as most others in the town.
Within, little or no difference exists from the simple
character of its exterior. It contains, however, a
goodly carved font. The present incumbent is
the Rev. Alderson.

At the lower end of St. Peter's street, and
adjoining the remains of Cardinal Wolsey's gateway, stands St. PETER's CHURCH, one of the largest
religious edifices in the town, but destitute of all
architectural embellishment. Within are the remnants of a few good gothic arches, which render it
probable that the church formed a portion of the
adjoining establishment of Wolsey, though this is
denied by some. The building contains a good
font of a very early character—probably Norman—and covered with carvings of animals extremely apocryphal in genus. During the incum-
bency of the present clergyman—the Rev. Mr.
Lumsden—the interior of the building has been
rendered somewhat convenient and ornamental.
The west end of the church has also been restored
to its legitimate use—an entrance—ingress having

been hitherto confined to a south porch and chancel door. The tower of St. Peter's is a good specimen of the peculiar flin work so frequently observed in the counties of Suffolk and Norfolk.

St. Stephen's Church is a small building, standing between St. Stephen's lane and Upper Brook street. The incumbent is the Rev. E. Harston. The western door of this church has also been appropriated to its proper use—the entrance hitherto being by a side porch. There are one or two interesting mediæval monuments in this building.

Stoke Church is the parochial church of the hamlet of Stoke, and is dedicated to St. Mary. A portion of the building is ancient. It lies on the opposite bank of the Gipping to that on which Ipswich stands, and is a picturesque object viewed from the town, by reason of the dense mass of timber which stands on the banks below it.

Among these edifices just mentioned there are none particularly large or affording much accommodation, neither are any of the incumbents burdened with excess of revenue. Indeed so small are the stipends of the clergy officiating in the Ipswich churches, that recourse was had to a special act of parliament for their increase as early as the days of Elizabeth. Under this act the churchwardens are empowered to ask of the town certain sums for the uses of the churches, and if no valid cause be shown to the contrary, the inhabitants of each parish are called upon by rate to furnish the necessary amount. The churches of

St. Mary at the Tower, St. Lawrence, and St. Mary Key, have usually had assistance granted them under this power.

By the munificence of the Rev. J. T. Nottidge, rector of St. Clement's and St. Helen's, a chapel of ease, dedicated to the HOLY TRINITY, has been built and opened for divine worship. The dense population residing in the upper part of the parish of St. Clement's rendered the necessity of affording more church room evident, and the highly respected incumbent was not slow in satisfying the spiritual wants of those who needed it. By the deed of endowment, the Rev. Mr. Nottidge not only gave the chapel free of expense for the uses of the parishioners, but also the sums of £1230, three per cent. consolidated bank annuities, and £1103 reduced bank annuities, with the interest, to be applied to the purpose of maintaining the officiating minister and repairing the church. The pew rents were also bestowed for the same purposes.

The construction of the church is plain and simple. It is eighty feet long by forty-eight wide, and twenty-five feet high; five windows on either side; surrounded on three sides with a gallery, under which are the free seats. It is said to contain about eight hundred persons. Externally, the chapel has nothing striking in its architectural ornaments; it is modest and unassuming, and its proportions are light. A portico shadows the entrance, above which is a small belfry, with one bell; this is surmounted by a cupola. The site is

well chosen, being upon an elevated spot ; and
from the roof is a full view of the borough, no
building approaching it. It adds much to the
improvement of the east end of the town. The
cost was about £2000. The whole was planned
and erected by Mr. Harvey, architect, of Carr-
street.

On the summit of the hilly ground upon the
turnpike road to Woodbridge, is a chapel erected
to the CATHOLIC faith. The present building is new
and stands upon the site of one of a far less pre-
tending character. The exterior is designed in the
early English style, but the contracted space upon
which it is built, rendering it necessary that the
details should be proportionably minute, it has
nothing very imposing in its appearance. The
interior is also of very contracted dimensions.
This sect is mainly indebted for the erection of
this new building to the efforts and the liberality
of the late Abbe Simon, who for a series of years
officiated as priest in the chapel. During the
lengthened residence of Abbe Simon, by his kindness of heart and cheerful disposition, he made
a large circle of friends and acquaintance, who on
various occasions testified the respect they held
towards him.

Dissenting places of worship are numerous in
Ipswich, the dissenting community being large,
wealthy, and highly respectable. The first building
perhaps in size as well as consequence is STOKE
CHAPEL, situated in the· hamlet of Stoke, and

belonging to a congregation of Baptists. The Rev. J. Sprigg, A. M. is the officiating minister. A building for divine worship was erected upon the spot occupied by the present chapel as far back as the year 1774, which has several times been enlarged in size, as the numbers attending increased. But little can be said in favour of the beauty of the structure, which is of octangular form, and entirely destitute of ornament both within and without. It is capable of accommodating nearly a thousand persons.

On the left hand side of St. Nicholas street, proceeding towards Stoke bridge, stands ST. NICHOLAS CHAPEL, dedicated to the use of Protestant Dissenters. It was opened for divine worship in 1829. The style of the building is gothic, and exists as an example of taste, which it would be well if followed by all the dissenting chapels in the town, upon every occasion of their enlargement or re-construction. The present minister is the Rev. J. Whitby.

In Globe lane, St. Matthew's—formerly called St. George's lane—stands a comparatively newly erected place of worship, named SALEM CHAPEL. The building was to a certain extent erected by the liberality of the late Mr. Joseph Chamberlain, a respectable inhabitant of the town, and the inventor of several salves and potions calculated to cure many ills to which flesh is heir. He was also the concoctor and dispenser of the renowned Dr. Sibley's solar tincture. Salem Chapel is small, not being capable of accommodating beyond five hundred persons. The present minister is the Rev. T. Middleditch.

TACKET STREET CHAPEL is situated in the street of that name, in the rear of a commodious open space. The building has rather an ancient appearance, though the date of its erection is 1720 only. The first congregation meeting within the walls came hither from a building in the Green Yard, St. Peter's, which they had used as a place of worship for forty years previously. The present building will seat between eight and nine hundred persons. It has a good organ. The Rev. W. Notcutt is the minister, the grandson of an eminent pastor of the same name, who also officiated at the chapel for many years, and died in 1756, at the good old age of eighty-four.

In DAIRY LANE is a small dissenting chapel under the care of the Rev. J. Nunn.

A small BAPTIST CHAPEL was erected in 1841, in St. Clement's parish, by seceders from Mr. Nunn's ministry.

The WESLEYAN METHODISTS own a commodious chapel in Old Gaol lane, now called New Market lane. The building is erected in the usual style of edifices intended for the performance of divine worship by the dissenting community, namely, plain in every feature, indeed we might almost say entirely destitute of ornament. The great object attempted to be attained is space and superior accommodation. The chapel in New Market lane is built for the accommodation of nine hundred persons, and was erected in the year 1816.

In consequence of an untoward dispute which arose between the Wesleyan Conference, and various communities once owning its sway, a number of Wesleyan dissenters in Ipswich, following the example set them by their brethren in various parts of England, seceded from the general body, and erected a chapel in Friars street. The chapel will hold five hundred persons. The foundation stone was laid the 6th of December, 1836, by Robert Eckett, Esq.

As the circumstances under which the chapel was erected mark an era in Wesleyanism, as well as the adornment of our town by the erection of a new place of worship, we record a few memoranda relative to the nature of the proceedings which followed on the occasion of laying the foundation. The inscription designed for the stone was as follows:

" This memorandum testifies, that a considerable number of Wesleyan Methodists in this town (as well as in many other places) having become separated from communion with the Wesleyan Conference, in consequence of the said Conference having enacted arbitrary and oppressive laws, in violation of the established rules of the society, as agreed to by the Conference and the people in the year 1797; for opposing these unrighteous proceedings, some of them have been unjustly expelled the society, and others of them, refusing to submit to unscriptural ecclesiastical domination, have withdrawn from communion with that body, and formed themselves into a society in connexion with the Wesleyan Methodist Association.

"A merciful Providence has opened a way for the erection of this chapel. Glory to God in the highest!

"The foundation stone was laid December 5th, Anno Domini 1836, by Robert Eckett, Esq., of London, with solemn prayer, and in pleasing hope that thousands of immortal souls may here be born from above, and finally, through the blood and righteousness of the Lord Jesus Christ, be called to partake of the inheritance of the saints in light. Amen, even so, Lord Jesus Christ! Hallelujah! the Lord God omnipotent reigneth.

C. Edwards,			Trustees,		J. Johnson,
E. Balls,			Preachers,		T. Norman,
J. Senton,	}		Leaders,	{	R. Boley,
H. Lovewell,			or		J. Cattermole,
R. Johnson,			Stewards.		T. Smith,

In the mayoralty of F. F. Seekamp, Esq.; James Morrison and Rigby Wason, Esqrs. being Members of Parliament for this borough of Ipswich."

Mr. Eckett, the gentleman who laid the stone, in the course of the day, entered into an explanation of the reasons of dissent from the body of Wesleyans in general, by comparing the laws of the society as they existed in the year 1797, and those of 1827, in which he showed that the Conference of the Society had unscripturally, despotically, and unecclesiastically, made new rules and regulations, which they had caused to be executed in a most unbecoming manner, by discharging respectable

individuals from the Society, merely on account of
" futile and trifling violations," as they were pleased
to call them. Mr. Eckett had, with many others,
without the consent of the Superintendent, called a
meeting to discuss the new rules, and on that very
account he was carried before the judge (who is the
superintendent) and his peers, and being arraigned
before them, he was found guilty. The mode of
proceeding was this :—The question as to the guilt
or innocence of the accused was first put to a show
of hands, and if there were two for and two against,
the fifth then gives the casting vote. Whether the
individual be acquitted or not, he is left in the
hands of the superintendent, who has power to
reverse the verdict at his pleasure, and who tells
him that in about one week he shall know his
doom; so that any individual thus circumstanced
has to be " *in terrorem*" of his judgment one
whole week, even after he may have received his
acquittal from the five travelling preachers. Mr.
Eckett designated this body, the New Star
Chamber. He then explained, at great length,
the rules and regulations of 1797, and contrasted
them with new ones made in 1827, and concluded
by saying, that he hoped and wished to make every
one of his audience feel that they had been
wronged, and that the liberty of the great reformation had been basely and unfeelingly wrung from
them by the Conference; and he sincerely hoped
that every person present would unite strongly to
get restored to them that liberty and those privi-

leges which were due to them, according to the rules and regulations of the late John Wesley, under whose banner he and they had enlisted.

Since this period, a third chapel of the same denomination of christians has been built, in the Rope Walk—a densely populated district, and where a place of worship was essentially required.

In a commodious, well-paved plot of ground, on the right hand side of St. Nicholas street, is situated the UNITARIAN CHAPEL. The building is old, and contains some good carving within it. The present officiating minister is the Rev. T. F. Thomas, a gentleman not less beloved by his flock, than highly esteemed by all who possess the pleasure of his acquaintance and the knowledge of his many talents and accomplishments.

Opposite the bank of Messrs. Alexanders', in Lower Brook street, stands the QUAKERS' MEETING House. It was built in 1706, and is calculated to contain eight hundred persons.

When we have named a small building used by the Jews as their synagogue, and situated in the Rope Walk, we shall have concluded the mention and description of buildings dedicated to the service of God existing in the town. Few places can boast of so large a number of churches and chapels, or of pulpits occupied by clergymen and ministers more zealous in their occupations than this town.

We now pass to buildings and institutions of a civil character.

EDIFICES APPROPRIATED TO THE ADMINISTRATION
OF JUSTICE.

The next building to which we shall advert, not
only as it regards its priority, but also its architectural characteristics, is the TOWN HALL, upon the
Corn-hill. Although bearing no comparison either
in dimensions or style with the new County Courts,
yet being more closely allied with the borough than
the latter building, we are therefore bound to
give it an earlier notice. The present Town-hall
was formerly the church of St. Mildred, which
stood upon the site, and was transmuted from its
religious to its civil character in an early era.
Indeed, to speak with closer approximation to truth,
the church, or a part of the old church, was used as
a Guild House for merchants, care being taken to
construct certain good and spacious kitchens for
the preparations of feasts which existed as proto-
types of those which followed in a more modern
era. The old Hall existed with little alteration
until the year 1818, when the ancient front, which
had a stair-case outside, was taken down, and the
present one erected. The interior also underwent
great alterations, and the whole building rendered
more commodious than our ancestors had made it,
and more in accordance with the increased importance of the town. The contemplated improvements were never however fully carried into effect;
and though a fair exterior presented itself to the

I

eye, the basement story, used as a place for
holding public meetings, was left unfinished until
the year 1841. The building however was rendered
tolerably commodious, and contained within it a
Council Chamber, well panelled and of spacious
dimensions, with a Police Office. Beyond these
apartments the accommodation was of a contracted
character, and inadequate to the purposes required.
The incompatibility of the place to the wants of
public business was endured through a series of
years until 1841, when, under the mayoralty of
Peter Bartholomew Long, Esq., the originator of
the improvements, the building assumed a new
internal aspect, and the wants of the town were
especially cared for.

These modern alterations, which might be styled
the completion of the building for long called-for
municipal purposes, have given on the ground floor
a Sessions' Hall, where prisoners convicted of
offences committed in the borough are tried under
the Recorder, Sir C. F. Williams, Knt., the present
chief judge of the Bankruptcy Court. The apartment is well lighted by a range of lofty windows,
and the public have the fullest accommodation the
area of space will allow. A stair-case from the
right of the seat of justice leads to the Council
Chamber, which has been remodelled out of the
old apartment set aside for that purpose, and is of
noble dimensions. The grand jury have also a
room devoted to their purposes, and various apartments are set apart for the use of the magistrates

and their officers. The Police Station is also within the building, and a range of strong cells are attached to this department on the ground level. Taken as a whole the alterations are of a very judicious nature.

The upper story of the Town-hall is used as the library and museum of the Ipswich Literary Institution, the accommodation being held of the corporation at a trifling rent. The Institution was established by shareholders, the object being to accumulate a good library for the benefit of the proprietors, and annual subscribers. A museum is also attached, containing many curious and rare specimens of natural history, as well as not a few treasures of art both native and foreign, and some interesting pieces of antiquity.

Besides an extensive library, a large collection of books formerly belonging to the corporation are deposited in the rooms. Of these we have spoken elsewhere. The history of this collection is in itself so singular, and includes in it so curious an episode, that we are tempted to give the narrative of its origin from a work published in 1747. We may premise that the relator of the story is most likely the party on whom the indignity of rejecting the label was passed.

"Mr. William Smart, portman, may be considered as the accidental founder of the public library; for it appears from a memorandum in the library, that his Latin books were not disposed of as he directed in his will, clause E, p. 37, but were kept in a chest,

till the year 1612, when they were deposited in
that spacious room in Christ's Hospital where they
now are: and though the value of these books and
manuscripts was not great, this legacy seems to
have put the corporation upon erecting a public
library, which otherwise perhaps they might not
have done. It is true, Mrs. Walter's legacy was
prior to Mr. Smart's, but whether she gave that
£50. to buy books for the library, or whether she
only gave the gross sum, and the corporation might
apply it as they thought fit, does not appear certainly, for we have not been able to learn where her
will was proved; but we rather think the latter was
the case, because, as the library was quite a new
thing to the town, it is likely that Mr. Bacon would
have taken notice of it in the following entry, where
he mentions this legacy, 36 Eliz. 1594. 'A treaty
was appointed with the Lord Mayor and his brethren,
by such as Mr. Bailiffs shall appoint, concerning
Mrs. Walter's gift, and the recovery of the same to
this town.' But whether it was Mrs. Walter or the
corporation that appropriated her £50. to this
commendable purpose, it was well done; and the
books bought with this money, added to Mr.
Smart's, made a considerable figure; so that, in
1612, the corporation thought proper to furnish the
room where they were kept with convenient presses,
for the security of these books, and for the reception of more. Most of these presses have been
filled with the generous gifts of benefactors; but
one or two are still empty, and are ready to receive

the gifts of any persons who are disposed to encourage learning in this town. The chamber adjoining to the library was once in part repaired by Mr. John Carnaby, who gave £3. towards it, but it is in so ruinous a condition at present, that there is not the least appearance that anything had ever been laid out upon it.

" There have been given to this library, between eight and nine hundred volumes, but some are lost; however, none within these last forty years : and this loss seems to have been the effect of carelessness rather than fraud ; for as we remember, Calvin's Institutions is almost the only book of any value among them. But though the books that are lost are not of great value, the loss of them should make the corporation more careful about the rest; hereafter we hope they will be so : at present little is to be expected, as the reader will judge from the following instance.

"A clergyman of this town, who had taken the trouble of examining every book in the library, observed, that though the name of the person who gave each book is written upon the title page of more than three-fourths of them, yet when the books are out of the library, and in the possession of a private person, there is nothing to show to what place they belong, nor to what use they were given. For though a book is said to be the gift of John a Noaks, it might as well be given by him to the person in whose possession it is, as to the Ipswich Library. He perceived likewise, that the

books were very likely to come into the hands of
private persons; for though the keys are commonly
lodged with the master of the Free-school, they are
often in the possession of the guide of Christ's
Hospital, who has twenty shillings a year for clean-
ing the room.   Therefore, as one probable means
of preventing any further embezzlement of the
· books, this clergyman, at his own expense, provided
a decent copper-plate, and caused a thousand copies
to be taken off, one of which he intended to have
cleaved upon the back of the title-page of each
book, that every one might know to what place
it belonged, and to what use it was given.   These
prints, and the plate, were intended by him as a
small gift to the library, and an earnest of more; he
not in the least doubting but every member of the
corporation would readily permit any other person
to take care of the library, though he might take no
care of it himself.   But some men, as it seems, will
neither do good themselves, nor suffer it to be done
by others; for intelligence being given of this
mischievous design, when the person employed to
paste on the prints came at the time previously
agreed upon, with the Rev. Mr. Hingeston the
School-master, the senior bailiff, who never had
them before, had the keys in his keeping; and the
answer was, ' that he would not part with them,
till he had consulted with some of the heads of the
corporation.'

"So the library was inspected, and a consultation
held, and the wise result of this was, that the print

should not be used; for all the members of this inspection, either concurred in opinion with the leader of it, or else acquiesced with what they had not power to prevent. If the donor of this plate had added another label to it, and said in words at length, this plate was given by ——— A. D. 1746, all pretence for objecting to it had been prevented; for this is no more than what is done to three-fourths of the gifts to this library : but he thought it would be a modester way of privately expressing that, if his arms were in miniature, added by way of embellishment to the plate; and well knowing that such sort of embellishments were by no means unusual in things of this nature, he had not the least suspicion that any person, let him be never so perverse, could be offended at it.

" But in this he was mistaken; for though none of the gentlemen who assisted at the consultation have favoured him with the reasons upon which they founded their determination, he has been told that they would seem to be offended at the addition of these arms. He has been credibly informed that one member of the inspection called this quartering his arms with those of the corporation; and whoever that was, he showed at once that he knew no more of arms than if he had been bred in a collier; and at the same time how liable a man is to blunder when he is inspecting what he does not understand.

" What the real motives were that induced the inspectors to reject the plate we are still to learn, but the reasons given by one of the consulted heads, who is supposed in effect to be the chief agent among them, were no better than these.

" 1. Because the date of the year is added to the plate, from whence it might be concluded that all the books were given in that year, 1746, whereas most of them were given long ago.

" 2. The print has not only the corporation arms, but those of the donor of it; if it were put into every book, it might be concluded from thence, nay, and it might be intended by him to insinuate, that the person who gave the plate, gave all the books in the library.

" So out of that strict and solemn regard which the two prime inspectors are known to have for truth, we are to suppose, they could not suffer the print to be used.

" That the reader may, at his leisure, sufficiently admire the sagacity of these reasons, the donor of the plate, (from whom we have had all that is here said about it) has presented him with a print of it; where, if he looks close, immediately under those of the corporation, he may discern these invidious arms; supported too, (such is the pride of this priest) by those no less deceitful figures 17 and 46.

"As to these harmless figures, upon the first glance of the print, you must perceive that the date is plainly no part of the label, and therefore would not be considered by an ordinary head as having any relation to the book or the giver of it, though they possibly may have some to the plate itself, and might be thought to signify that it was given in the very year represented by those figures. But a man who knows nothing of figures is very apt to be disgusted at the sight of them.

" As to the second reason, the donor of the plate begs leave to observe, that the arms of the late Earl of Dysart are affixed to a beam in the Church of St. Lawrence, Ipswich, in memory of his having given the parishioners some timber when they repaired the roof of it; but, he believes, that the most simple fellow that has seen them there, did never conclude from thence that the late Lord Dysart built the church, though there is not a single word added to prevent him from making that conclusion. In like manner it is apprehended by many persons less sagacious than the inspectors, that this print might safely have been trusted in the books of the library without any danger of its being thought that the owner of these arms, in 1746, gave all the books, any more than it is thought that my Lord Dysart built St. Lawrence Church.

" But as it is difficult exactly to know what conclusions may be made by the perverseness of man, if care be not taken to prevent it; it happens luckily in the present case, that all possibility of any such danger as the inspectors would be thought to discover, is effectually prevented by the label at the bottom of the print, the blank part of which was evidently intended to be filled up with the name of the person who gave each particular book.

" As these reasons then are so childish and

ridiculous, that they could not influence any sensible man, no nor (to use the polite language of the Ipswich-levee) the greatest fool that ever lived; and as the consulted head that uttered them, is known not to want common understanding, the reader is left to judge whether these were the real reasons, or whether they were only the weak and lame pretence for insulting this clergyman, either because he was supposed to have some concern in publishing this account of these charities, or for some other reasons of too personal a nature to be here mentioned.

" We ask pardon of the reader for detaining him so long about so trifling a concern, and proceed in our undertaking. We think we need say nothing to recommend this particular charity, for the great usefulness of public libraries is seen at first sight, as they do so evidently tend to the advancement of useful knowledge and learning, by putting it into the power of the studious to peruse many books, which otherwise they might not have ability or opportunity of purchasing. And that they may the longer continue to answer this good end, in regulating them, two things ought principally to be considered. 1. That all proper persons may have an easy access to the books. 2. That this be permitted in such a manner that the public may not thereby be made liable to suffer by the embezzlement of them. With a view to both these, the following proposals are offered to the consideration of those whom it may concern.

" 1. That a lock be provided for every press, so that the room may be cleaned by the servants of the hospital, without their being allowed to come at the books.

" 2. That an exact catalogue be taken of all the books, and a duplicate taken of it, one to be kept in the treasury, the other in the library.

" 3. That a proper person be appointed by the corporation to be library-keeper, who should give security for the books intrusted with him, and be answerable for any deficiency. And it is presumed that any person who shall be thought a proper master of the Grammar School, will always be a proper person to be intrusted with the care of the library.

" 4. That the library-keeper be empowered to lend any of the books to any person that he shall think proper, at his discretion ; but that he should be answerable for all the books so lent by him.

" 5. That either of the bailiffs, any portman, or common-council-man, be authorised to take any book for his own use, and to order the delivery of any book or books to such person or persons as he shall think proper, by warrant under his hand to the library-keeper, which warrant should be a dis-charge for those books; and the person by whom the warrant is drawn should be answerable for the books delivered by virtue of the said warrant until they be returned.

" 6. That every person taking, or borrowing any book, should give the library-keeper a receipt for

' it, which receipt should be re-delivered upon the return of the book.

"7. That the library-keeper should keep a book, in which he should enter an account of all books lent by him, taken by any of the bailiffs, portmen, or common-council-men, or delivered by their warrants, specifying the time when, and the person to whom, each book is delivered, and the time when it is returned.

"8. That a small annual salary be appointed to the library-keeper, for his trouble, (five or six pounds might be sufficient) which salary might be paid out of the profits of Mr. Smart's estate, or Tooley's.

"We apprehend that some such regulations as these would effectually prevent any further loss : and we doubt not but the library would flourish, and soon receive sufficient encouragement from the public, if gentlemen were to see their gifts were properly disposed of, and a proper care were taken of them.   But these are submitted to the public as short hints, and as a rough sketch of what might be improved and amended."

The Corn-hill, upon the south side of which the Town Hall stands, was not until comparatively late years the wide open space it is at present.   Formerly the Market Cross, and a heap of buildings called the Rotunda, stood upon the spot.   The Cross was taken down about 1812, though its demolition was accompanied with many compunctious visitings by many of the old inhabitants, who looked upon it as a sacred portion of the buildings of the town, and that without it the borough could not exist in prosperity. The feelings which prompted this attachment to the old thing of wood and stone were indeed laudable and praiseworthy. Historical remembrances, of no common kind, were attached to it. It had been erected by that great benefactor to Ipswich, Edmund Daundy, in 1510, and had been beautified and kept in repair by the patriotism of those who looked upon its comeliness and soundness as matters that concerned all. Edward Daundy was the relative of Wolsey, and therefore the Cross in some degree kept alive the memory of that great man in the minds of his townsmen. Rejoicings of no common character had taken place at the Cross upon political occasions, from the time of the Restoration downward. Proclamations had been rehearsed from its base, and at earlier eras preachings had been made from the cross. These events and these connections exalted the old building above merely common interest. A local poet thus beautifully apostrophizes this departed relic :—

> " The old Cross
> Stood on the market-hill ; alas ! our loss,
> That never saw it there ; it is too poor
> This age of ours, in fashioners,—to endure
> That the rich fabrics of those cunning hands
> The old time guided, like the shapeless sands
> Should fall, and fall, and fall,—and not a care
> Be felt to stay the ruin, or to spare
> That which decay makes beautiful.''

The COUNTY COURTS in which the sessional
business of the county is transacted and the Assizes
held, are situated in front of the County Gaol, in
St. Helen's parish.   The building is quite new,
having been erected in 1836-7, in consequence of
the dilapidated condition and incommodious nature
of the Old Shire-hall, which formerly stood on a
plot of land in Foundation Street, called the Shire-
hall Yard.

The building is two hundred and fifty feet long,
and fifty feet deep.   In the centre of the north front
is the chief entrance to the prison; to the east or
right of it is the Criminal Court, for the trial of
prisoners: this chamber is 45 feet long and 30
feet wide, with 20 feet between the ceiling and
floor; at one end of it is the bench for the judges;
opposite, a gallery for strangers; in the centre
is the dock for the prisoners on their trial.
This communicates by a passage passing beneath
the flooring of the Court with the Gaol, so
that the prisoners are brought immediately from
the prison yard into the dock, without having
occasion to wait in Court, and be immediately conveyed back by the same subterraneous means.   The
centre of the Court is adapted to the usual purposes,
for counsel, attorneys, &c., and lighted by windows
from the top, understood by the name of lanterns.
Next to this is a small room for witnesses ; above
which is a private chamber for counsel to confer
with them ; beyond is the counsels' chamber.   At
the extreme east is a room for the magistrates,

being lighted by five large windows, and is full as large as the Criminal Court. To the left of the entrance, being the west wing, which corresponds in size with the east wing already described, is the Nisi Prius Court, and witnesses' room, with a private chamber above; contiguous is a room for the records, and another for the weights and measures, and lastly, one at the extreme point of the building, which is of exactly the same dimensions as that for the magistrates at the east end, for the grand jury, which is also lighted by five windows. At the N. E. and N. W. points is a tower, each thirty feet high. To the right and left entrance are two other towers, being forty feet in height, between which and over the entrance is the judges' private chamber, which is approached by a stair-case running within the interior of the left tower. The right tower forms a room for the clerk of the peace. The entrances to the two Courts, are by private doors, being between them and the witnesses' chamber. The front has six windows at the extremity of each wing, which are of oblong form, opened by sashes. At the east and west fronts, are three windows of the same dimensions, and a small one in each of the centre towers. The walls of the Courts have on the east side, carved on stone, the royal arms, and on the west the county arms. The building is in the Tudor style of architecture. It is constructed of the best Suffolk white brick, the base and copings being of stone. The whole front stands at an elevation of about thirty feet.

Eminent in each department of the law, every case, criminal or civil—whether involved in the intricacies of legal labyrinths, or falling under some new form of statute—act of parliament, or recent decision, will, in the members of the Suffolk bar, find able expounders and masters. Nor is it possible that in any particular case, the whole talent of the Suffolk bar should be monopolized by plaintiff or defendant, in retaining one or two of the most eminent barristers. If the attorney of a plaintiff pick his men, there are plenty left possessed of equal ability, from which the adviser of the defendant can make an unexceptionable selection. The quality and quantity of talent is well balanced, and every suitor at the bar of justice will find abundant and able advocates to support his claim.

The building was erected by contract by Mr. Lake, at the sum of £6149. Only two contracts were sent in, the other being from Messrs. Hearsum and Denham of this town for £6920, which being the highest was of course rejected. The architect was M'Brook, Adelphi, London.

It was not until the summer of 1839 that the holding of the assizes of the county were divided alternately between Bury St. Edmund's and Ipswich. Applications had been made at various periods for leave to hold either the spring or summer assizes here, but without effect. At length through the unremitting exertions of Rigby Wason, Esq., M.P. for the borough, aided and assisted by Fitzroy Kelly, Esq., the removal was consummated, and on the fifth of August, 1839, the first assizes were held in Ipswich.

In order to show the unfair advantages held by the western side of Suffolk over the eastern, with regard to the holding of the assizes, it would be only necessary to give a statement of the comparative population between the two divisions of the county. Yet this injustice was perpetrated for years—compelling suitors and their witnesses to travel from one extremity of Suffolk to another, when they might have been accommodated at half the distance. The same might be said of grand jurymen, and the local legal profession.

At the rear of the assize courts stands the COUNTY GAOL, a building replete with every convenience and plan of safety for the custody of prisoners. It is under the able governorship of Mr. E. A. Johnson. The County Gaol was erected about 1786, upon the site of an ancient burial ground, and was one of the earliest constructed upon the enlightened and benevolent views of the celebrated John Howard. It is many years since an execution of any criminal confined in this gaol took place, and sincerely is it to be hoped that succeeding years will pass on to an indefinite period, and find the town unpolluted by the disgusting and crime-inducing spectacle of a public execution.

The BOROUGH GAOL is situated in the Borough Road, a populous street in the rear of the County Gaol. This building is of course less capacious

K

and less imposing in its exterior than the gaol
appropriated to county offenders. It has a strong
front graced with the usual appendage of fetters
in effigy, and the interior, by alterations made
pursuant to the recommendations of the government
commission for the inspection of the gaols of the
kingdom, is rendered as safe and convenient as
confined space will allow. As, however, the borough
enlarges in population, this building will be found
incompetent to contain the number of offenders
multiplying with the increase of people. A new
building must, sooner or later, be erected, and it is
to be hoped that when that time arrives, the magistrates will decide upon some more eligible site than
that in which the present building stands.

The OLD SHIRE HALL, of which cursory mention
has been made, stood until the month of October,
1841, within a large plot of ground called the Shire
Hall Yard, in Foundation Street. The building
was of the plainest character—plain not only with
regard to its simplicity, but also in the common
acceptation of the word—ugly. It had no second
story, the whole of the apartments being upon the
ground floor. These consisted of two ill-arranged
courts for the transaction of public business, and
two smaller apartments, in one of which the weekly
petty sessions of the county magistrates were held.
Upon occasions of holding the quarter sessions, one
of the larger apartments was used. The building
was not however deserted, until it became apparent
that if used for any purpose much longer, the

ceiling would some day tumble down upon jury, prisoner, populace, and recorder. Some disputes have arisen between the corporation and the charity commissioners of the borough, as to which body held legal title to the building—the latter claiming certain interests which the corporation do not recognise.

Within the same area stands the OLD BRIDE-WELL and CHRIST'S HOSPITAL. The buildings connected with this institution lie on the north-east side of the Shire Hall Yard, and originally formed a portion of the establishment of the Black Friars, and a portion of the cloisters belonging to this religious community still exists upon the premises, as perfect and fresh as when trodden by the monks of old, of whose possessions they formed a part.

Christ's Hospital was to a certain extent founded by the corporation, who purchased the buildings called the Bridewell of the Friars' preachers, and gave them to the purposes of the charity. The object of the establishment of Christ's Hospital was twofold—" Curing the sick and the correction of the vicious." Its main support originally was by voluntary contribution, but it gradually became endowed with funds, with which other small charities were consolidated, and from which it now derives a good revenue. The corrective part of the charity has fallen for some considerable period into disuetude, and the school, no longer confined within its old boundaries, is removed to a handsome and convenient erection upon the Stoke road, near the Union-house.   K 2

In order to understand the real nature of the original institution, we extract the following information from the charter of the hospital, by which the real object will be seen.

" *Elizabeth, D. G. &c.* Whereas our faithful and beloved subjects the bailiffs, &c. of Ipswich, in our county of Suffolk, moved (as it becomes those who sincerely profess the Gospel and the Christian religion) with an honest and laudable zeal of charity, not only commiserating the poor, the aged, the orphans, the widows, the sick, and others that are in want; but also induced by their prudent regard for the common weal, to correct the vagrants and vagabonds begging without real necessity, who are the lazy drones of the commonwealth, and the seminary [*Seminarium*] of thieves, have built and prepared several houses, structures, and edifices, upon their own ground within the town of Ipswich aforesaid, at their own proper costs and charges; and have fitted and furnished them with necessaries; and have endowed them with perpetual funds, possessions, and provisions; and have determined to endow them more amply and liberally in time to come; and for ever to preserve and maintain them with this intention, viz. that in the said houses care might be taken of, and provision made for, (1.) the poor and orphans, especially such as are very young or very aged, who can of themselves have no livelihood and honest education, that they may not be unmercifully left to perish, to the great scandal of the Christian religion; or be accustomed to base idleness, and evil practices, and brought up to the greater detriment of the commonwealth: and that (2.) such as sickness renders unuseful to themselves and the public, so that, though they were never so willing, they could not support themselves, may by this means be piously cured, and preserved alive for honest uses; and lastly, (3.) that they whose age and health renders them strong enough for lawful employments, may neither for want of them apply themselves to theft and evil practices; nor yet dishonestly and idly strolling, divert the alms of those who are really poor, [*vere pauperum Elee-mosynam;*] or be suffered to endanger good people; but being busied in honest employments, may both maintain themselves, and be compelled to be useful to the commonwealth. And whereas our aforesaid beloved and faithful subjects the bailiffs, &c. of Ipswich, have most gratefully set forth, that they have received not only all their riches (which they acknowledge themselves to enjoy by the blessing of peace and of our protection) but also the knowledge of the true religion; and these fruits of that, the pious commiseration of the exigencies of their brethren, under God, from us and our ministry, and for that reason have most humbly besought us that we would condescend to approve this their com-mendable purpose, to promote it, and take it into our protection; and lastly, as a mark of their grati-tude towards us [*in ipsorum grati animi erga nos signum*] to distinguish and call it by such name and title as we should think proper. We, consenting to

their humble petition, of our especial grace, certain
knowledge, and mere motion, as much as in us
lieth, have approved, confirmed, and ratified, this
their pious and laudable institution ; and do take it
into the royal patronage, defence, and protection, of
us, our heirs and successors ; and in remembrance
of our approbation, confirmation, and ratification;
and for a perpetual testimony how pleasing such
pious deeds are to us, and how much we desire to
exhort and animate our other subjects (who have it
·equally in their power and ability) to show forth the
like fruits of the Gospel, and to imitate so good a
work, to the honour of the supreme King and of
our Saviour Christ, whose members will there be
mercifully and piously taken care of ; of our especial grace, and of our certain knowledge, and mere
motion, and by the supreme plenitude and power of
our royal prerogative [*suprema prerogativæ nostræ
regalis plenitudine et potestate,*] we will, that the
houses, structures, edifices, and funds, to be applied
to the uses aforesaid, be by all for ever called and
named Christ's Hospital, in our town of Ipswich."

Since the passing of the Municipal Corporation
Act, and the consequent re-modelling of the
government of local charity boards, this institution
has been not only resuscitated, but new and
increased usefulness added to its former condition.
The school has been removed, as previously stated,
to a building connected with the charities, and
almost rebuilt for the purpose, near the Union
House in the parish of Stoke. Here no less than

forty boys are educated, clothed, lodged, fed, and apprenticed at suitable ages to such trades and employments as may be agreed upon, or that might suit the capacities of the children. Instead of the paltry sum formerly paid to the master, a handsome stipend is allowed to a competent person to educate and superintend the scholars. This change in the management of the school was effected by the local charity trustees in 1841. The school of Christ's Hospital might now be reckoned one of the most useful charitable institutions of which the town can boast.

We have digressed somewhat from the main subject—the Old Bridewell—and now return to it. As before stated, this building was formerly a part of the convent occupied by the Friars' preachers, and some very perfect remains of the cloisters attached to the establishment are extant within the walls. They consist of a widely-paved walk upon the ground floor and a gallery above, surrounding a grass plot. The pillars and gallery are timber. On the upper story, at the east and west ends, a rude desk is fixed, used, it is presumed, by the preachers of the monastery when they addressed its inmates. The same contrivance has also been used for the purposes of the school in later days. On the south side of the building are the cells, of roomy dimensions, and well supplied with air. During the alterations at the Town-hall, they have been used for the temporary imprisonment of parties under custody of the police. The exterior of the building is of a more modern character than parts of its interior. Above one of the porches stood an effigy of a Christ Church school boy, arrayed in appropriate costume. This has been removed to the new school house.

MILITARY BUILDINGS.

Ipswich is a garrison town, and possesses as convenient a set of cavalry barracks, situated in as healthy a situation, as any building of the same kind in the kingdom. They are erected at the upper end of St. Matthew's street, and contain within the walls a fine open space of ground, of sufficient dimensions for the exercise of a regiment of horse. At the higher end of the space stand houses for the accommodation of the officers—non-commissioned officers—and at the wings, lodging rooms for the privates and stables for horses. The magazine, armourer's shop, tailor's shop, canteen, &c, stand at the lower end. The town of Ipswich benefits largely by the military stationed here. Independently of the liberal and fair dealing of both officers and men, the barracks being head-quarters, the presence of a military staff accompanied by a good band, imparts a gaiety to the town which is at least both agreeable and enlivening.

In the times of war, now happily past and gone, the town of Ipswich was an important depot for the military. Its proximity to the European coast, and its contiguity with Harwich, then the port from

whence the continental packets connected with
government took their departure, rendered it extremely convenient for the residence of a large
body of the army, who could, as circumstances
required, be shipped off to the scene of warfare
with regularity and dispatch. It is calculated that
in the height of the last war, not less than twelve
or fourteen thousand troops were barracked and
billeted in the town. A line of barracks extended
on the Stoke side of the New Quay; and also
upon the Woodbridge road, immediately below the
opening of the road to St. Helen's, barracks were
erected, the remnants of which—temporary dwellings as they were—yet remain to attest the fact.
These hovels (for by no other name can the houses
now be called) have been rendered, by their dilapidated and filthy condition, an eyesore and nuisance
to the neighbourhood. In this age of improvement
and the extension of building, surely some specu-
lator could be found ready to relieve the locality
of so unsightly a remnant, and erect upon their
area such buildings as the want and taste of the
times require.

In almost all the churchyards of the town, lie
interred the remains of many of those unfortunate
heroes, who returned with shattered constitutions
from the disastrous expedition to Walcheren.
Report says that so intensely anxious were these
miserable creatures to regain the shores of England, that large numbers were landed from the
ships which brought home the miserable remnant,

along the whole Suffolk and Essex coast. But few,
however, reached the hoped-for destination of their
earthly homes. Exhausted nature had sunk too
low for renovation. These men dropped by the
wayside and in villages as they dragged themselves
along. A large body reached Ipswich, and the
churchyards were so often called upon to receive
their ashes, that in one or two burial grounds a
spot was specially set apart for their interment.

In 1839 a fracas took place between the privates
of the Fourth Dragoon Guards, commanded by
Lieut. Colonel Chatterton, and the police, in which
several of the latter were much beaten and wounded.
An unpleasant feeling was engendered between the
military and civil power upon the first evening of
the entrance of the former into the town, when a
disturbance taking place in a public-house on the
Woodbridge road, a police inspector took one of
the soldiers into custody, who violently and dan-
gerously assaulted him in the cell. This first outbreak led to a state of bad feeling between the two
bodies, until at length the disturbances became so
frequent and of such magnitude, that General Sir
Charles D'Albiac was sent down from the Horse
Guards to be present at an investigation of the
whole matter before the magistrates. A volumi-
nous body of evidence was collected and transmitted to the military authorities in London, but no
decision followed.

LIBRARIES.

Ipswich contains several good libraries. The Ipswich PUBLIC LIBRARY is situated in the Butter Market, at the house of Mr. Pawsey, bookseller, who is the librarian of the society.

The Ipswich LITERARY INSTITUTION has its library and museum at the Town Hall—a full account of which has been given in the history of the Town Hall and of Christ's Hospital.

There are but few towns in England which can boast the possession of a more extensive and better chosen library than that attached to the Ipswich MECHANICS' INSTITUTION, in Tavern Street. Upwards of 3,000 volumes of useful and agreeable knowledge are to be found ranged upon its shelves. The members of the Institution are numerous and rapidly increasing, and the benefits conferred by it on the mechanics of the town are incalculable.

The first meeting towards the establishment of a Mechanics' Institution took place in the year 1824, at the Town Hall, when such was the unanimous state of feeling in favour of such an institution, that upwards of one hundred persons gave in their names as members. After such an exhibition of feeling on behalf of an object, it must readily be supposed that a Mechanics' Institute was soon formed. From that time to the present it has continued to flourish, and let us hope that its sphere of usefulness and enjoyment may continue to enlarge.

The building in which the Institute is held contains a spacious lecture room, library, museum, committee rooms, and other apartments all admirably adapted to the purpose.

STREETS—CHRIST CHURCH HOUSE AND PARK—MR. SPARROWE'S HOUSE, ETC.

The visitor will be competent to judge for himself of the convenient width, perfect paving, and parallelism of the streets of Ipswich, without directing them to his attention. It might be said, however, that although the modern genius of improvement has not yet visited numerous places, thoroughfares, lanes and alleys of the town, yet much of that narrow and tortuous character they have hitherto borne has been removed. Of course in whatever parts the inducements of private speculation, or of public benefit, have led to the erection of new streets, the wants of the public, in wider road-ways and foot-paths, have been considered. Until within a few years back, no new streets have been built; but from the year 1838, a new town—as indeed the numerous houses might be called, erected on the site of a well-known piece of ground, called "Bird's Garden"—has arisen on the south-west. A line of goodly habitations have within the same period been built upon the Norwich Road, standing upon a site intended to be made the locality of a suburb of elegant character, accommodated with its own church, and other public conveniences. The merit of the design is due to Mr. I. M. Clarke, architect,

ANCIENT HOUSE, IPSWICH. THE RESIDENCE OF J. E. SPARROWE, ESQ.

though for private reasons the speculators have not carried it into execution.

While in some measure calling attention to the high-ways and social buildings of the town, we must not omit to direct the observation of the stranger to a curious antique house standing in the Butter Market, known by the name of MR. SPARROWE'S HOUSE, the residence of J. E. Sparrowe, Esq. We subjoin the following full description from "The Historic Sites of Suffolk."

"There is perhaps no house in the kingdom, which for its size, is more curiously or quaintly orna-mented, or contains within its apartments more that can interest the connoisseur in fine paintings—the student in genealogy—or the lover of antiquity. The architect of the building is unknown, but it was believed to have been built for the residence of Mr. Robert Sparrowe, in 1567, by an individual named Clyatt. It has however been discovered within a few years, that in the year 1570, the build-ing was occupied by George Copping, and by him erected in 1567. This information is contained in the will of Mrs. Joan West, made about that date, widow of William West, who in demising the Wag-gon Inn, still the next house to Mr. Sparrowe's, describes her own tenement to stand between G. Copping's house upon the west, and the tenement of — Ward, where one Ralph Carrawaye now dwell-eth, on the east; whose north head abutteth on the Fish Market Street, and the south head thereof on the churchyard of St. Stephen. Added to this

evidence, the initials of G. Copping exist upon
the door-way, and over the mantel-piece of an inner
room of the building; and being accompanied by
the figures, 1567, are presumed to mark not only
the name of the builder, but also the date of the
erection of the building.

"The exterior of the house is unique. The basement front is finely carved in strings of pendant
fruit.

"On the second story there are four bay windows
in the front—which is about seventy feet next the
street; and on the base of each of these windows
are respectively sculptured the emblematical figures
of Europe, Asia, Africa, and America, with their
peculiar attributes. Above the windows is a considerable projection, extending the whole length of
the front, forming a promenade, on the outside,
nearly round the house. On the roof are four attic
windows, forming so many gable ends, and corres-
ponding with those beneath them. Over these upper
windows are figures of Cupids in different attitudes:
and the whole exterior of the building is profusely
ornamented with animals, fruit, and flowers, with
wreaths of roses and other devices relative to the
armorial bearings of the Sparrowe family. No
chimnies can be seen from the street. On the west
end of the house, facing St. Stephen's Lane, is
represented an uncouth figure of Atlas with a long
beard, kneeling on one knee, and supporting the
globe on his shoulders. At the corner, a little below
this is a pastoral scene; consisting of a figure sitting

under a tree surrounded by sheep : another figure,
a shepherd, is approaching him, with his hat in one
hand, and a crook, which projects from the wall, in
the other; he is leading a flock of sheep; and is in
the attitude of addressing the person who is seated
beneath the wide-spreading beech. It is not, however, easy to determine from the foliage, whether
the tree is meant for a beech, an oak, or an elm ;
but there is little doubt but that the artist, being
seized with a fit of classical enthusiasm, intended
this effort as an illustration of the discourse between
Tityrus and Meliboeus, in the first eclogue of Virgil.

" We are induced to believe that the ornaments on
this house are all emblematical; and we may infer,
from this last composition, that the wool trade then
flourished in Ipswich, and was of great importance;
and the other decorations in front are intended to
imply that it was carried on with all quarters of the
globe.

"The interior of this singular structure contains
several extremely fine rooms. The dining room is
closely panelled in dark oak, carved in a manner
which would do honour even to the great genius of
Grinling Gibbons. The fire-place, furnishing capacious chimney corners, exhibits the finest parts of
the carver's skill, in wreaths of vine and pendant
fruits. In the centre protrudes a strong bas relief
of the arms and crest of the Sparrowe family, and
on each side are panels inlaid in fanciful designs,
with wood of a lighter colour than their ground
work. A door to the right of the fire-place also

exhibits some fine inlaying and carving, and the beams of the room, an unusual circumstance, are as deeply chiselled as any part of the wainscot. The dimensions of this room are twenty-two feet by twenty-one, and although the apartment is, by reason of a low ceiling, and its dark lining, rather sombre to the eye, yet unquestionably in its *tout ensemble*, it is one of the finest rooms of its size, to be found in any house in Ipswich. Upon the first floor spreads an apartment more fitting for the mansion of a nobleman than the residence of a private individual. It extends over the whole of the front part of the house. The ceiling is traversed by heavy oak beams, and divided into compartments ornamented by ponderous wreaths of fruit. The corners are filled with shields, containing the crests of the family. The dimensions of the room are forty-six feet by twenty-one feet. In this apartment hang several old paintings, to one of which is attached a tradition, that the individual whom it represents was, for his extreme cruelty to the Protestants, consumed alive by vermin. The manner in which this extraordinary retributive death is believed to have taken place is not known, nor indeed do those ancient members of the family who were the last recipients of the related miracle, profess to be acquainted with the exceeding crimes which even roused the creeping things of the earth to make war against and devour the persecutor. The name of this obnoxious individual is Gosnall. If we may be allowed to judge of his character, by the benign

repose thrown by the painter into the countenance
of this monstrous traditional offender, history has
much defamed him. The resemblance is that of a
quiet old man, more desirous of enjoying silence
and repose in his descent to the grave, than coun-
selling and conducting persecution against any
sect, as an amusement of his declining years. He
appears habited in a blue dress sitting close to his
figure. Next to this picture hangs a singular portrait of James the First, painted in the first year of
his reign. The extremes of meanness, cunning, and
duplicity appear to mingle in the countenance of
the Scottish inheritor of the British throne. Judg-
ing from this portrait, it may be safely said, that if
James did really penetrate the horrible mystery of
the Gunpowder conspiracy, that the English Parliament were indebted for its safety more to the
cunning of the " canny" King than his boasted
wisdom. It may be a curious question for historical
physiologists to decide, why it happens that James,
the child of two most beautiful persons—Mary
Queen of Scots and Henry Earl of Darnley, should
have possessed features so ordinary, and an expression of countenance so repugnant, as that in which
painters uniformly represent him. In a bed chamber adjoining this room, the ornaments of the
ceiling are changed—fleur-de-lis being substituted
for the usual garlands of fruit, and the family badges.
No reason can be assigned for the alteration, but
the difference is not thought to have arisen solely
from the taste of the ancient proprietor. A small

L

door in one corner of the large apartment opens
upon a staircase leading to the roof of the house,
from which issues a door-way to the leads over the
wide eaves of the building. These leads are sufficiently wide to afford a safe promenade, and every
part of the upper portion of the building can be
reached by them.   In the year 1801, a singular discovery was made in this upper story of the house,
being nothing less than a concealed loft, without
doubt forming the roof of a chapel, the body of
which existed in a room immediately beneath. The
existence of this apartment was discovered by the
merest accident, the connection between the loft,
being separated by a built-up wall.   Time and
damp however, displacing a portion of the plaster,
the light of day found its way through the cranny,
and the place was discovered.   The arched timbers
of a slightly ornamented roof exist within it, and at
the time of its being opened the floor was strewed
with wooden angels and such figures as usually
serve to decorate a catholic oratory. It is supposed
that the chapel existed in a perfect state, at the date
of the Reformation, but after that period, the open
assumption of the proscribed faith becoming dangerous, the body of this place of worship was
converted into a common sitting room, and the
roof concealed by a beamed ceiling.

"There exists in the Sparrowe family, a tradition
descending from father to son, that through the
agency of one of its members, a zealous loyalist,
Charles the Second lay sometime concealed within

this house after the battle of Worcester. Previously
to the discovery of the secret room, some difficulty
had arisen with regard to the locality of the hiding
place of the royal fugitive, but the opening of· this
chamber seems to point to its solution. It is but
fair to add that the family are not in possession of
any documentary evidence proving the residence of
Charles within the habitation, but there is apparently
a close, yet mysterious connection existing between
the Sparrowe family and the then reigning House
of Stuart, which might have been of the kind to
which allusion has been made. Several portraits
of Charles the Second are in possession of the
Sparrowes; as also of other members of that branch
of the Stuarts. The arms of Charles stand on the
exterior of the front of the house, conspicuously
emblazoned; and two portraits of the monarch, and
one of Mrs. Lane, are sacredly kept by a member
of the family to the present day, as memorials from
the hand of Charles himself, upon leaving the
place. The fact of one of these miniatures being a
likeness of Mrs. Lane, the heroic deliverer of the
monarch from the perils of captivity, is, we con-
ceive, a proof added to other evidences of the
probability, that partaking the protection of the
Sparrowe family, Charles sent them his likeness,
with that of a fellow contributor to his safety, as an
appropriate remembrance of their peculiar service.
This Mrs. Lane was a maiden lady, in the house of
whose brother, at Bentley, in Staffordshire, Charles
the Second took refuge, and was conveyed by her—

Charles being put in the disguise of a servant—from that place to Bristol. Had Charles presented the likeness of any other lady to the Sparrowes, the chain of connection would have been broken. His gift however being the likeness of one distinguished by the performance of an heroic act for his safety, it was a proper token of remembrance to be transmitted to a person who had befriended him in equally perilous circumstances. There are no records existing, that we have found, stating Charles ever to have been driven to Ipswich, or even into Suffolk, during his misfortunes. The neighbouring counties, however, boast of receiving him ; and first and last, he was indebted to upwards of forty persons for the preservation of his life during his eventful wanderings. Besides the two miniatures spoken of, the present possessor of the house in the Butter Market, Ipswich, holds a beautiful miniature of Charles the First, enclosed in a locket, also presented to his family.

The premises and grounds of this singular mansion, formerly extended some distance down St. Stephen's lane, as indeed is to be collected from Johan West's will, which expresses, that they abut upon the churchyard of St. Stephen. The old Turret garden and bowling green formed a portion of the grounds attached, and were laid out as an orchard and shrubbery, diversified with gravel walks.

There exists an absurd rumour, that this property, in consequence of a peculiar devise, cannot be held,

or the house inhabited, by any other person than
one bearing the name of "John Sparrowe." The
report has not the slightest foundation in truth,
and it is presumed arises from the circumstance
that after the sale of the property by G. Copping,
to R. Sparrowe, in 1573, it has been inhabited by
the Sparrowe family only. This Robert Sparrowe
was son and heir of John Sparrowe, of Somersham,
and served the office of Portman of Ipswich.
Among other valuable paintings in this house are
the following.

Portrait of Charles the Second, by Vandyke.
This painting is a *chef d'œuvre* of the real
master.

A sketch of a gigantic figure, armed cap a pie,
said to represent John Sparrowe, slain at the battle
of Hexham on the part of Henry the Sixth.

A portrait by Gainsborough, of John Sparrowe,
thirteen times bailiff of Ipswich.

Father of the above painted by Sir Peter Lely.

The great grandfather of the present John Ed-
dowes Sparrowe. This ancient gentleman was
parent to thirty-two children. The painting is
said to be by the hand of Sir Peter Lely.

An old lady of the family, name unknown.

Portrait of Judge Clench, of the Court of Common Pleas, who married Dorcas Sparrowe. The
original of the portrait lies interred in Holbrook
church. Hollar's engraving of the Judge is taken
from this picture. The painter is Holbein.

Sir John Sparrowe, Knight of the Green Cloth,

in the reign of James the Second, by Sir Godfrey Kneller.

Captain Robert Sparrowe, Captain of the Train Bands; the figure wears a Puritan dress.

On the stair-case hangs a full length portrait of George the First, by G. Fountaine, 1727, presented by the monarch, to John Sparrowe, bailiff of Ipswich, in return for attentions received during his visit to Ipswich from Mr. Sparrowe, and the presentation of a huge sweet cake called a March-pane.

On an upper landing place hangs a likeness of Henrietta Maria, consort of Charles the First, by Vandyke.

A portrait of Villiers, Duke of Buckingham.

The present possessor of this interesting mansion has in his possession, a descent of his family, commencing in the year 1419, with Thomas Sparrowe, de Somersham in com Suffolk.

It appears that the ancestors of the Sparrowe family were as anxious that their last and " narrow house" should be as snug and comfortable as that they inhabited when living. In Saint Lawrence Church, on the entrance to the family vault, are inscribed the following words :

" NIDUS PASSERUM."

Another building of far greater importance, though not in curiosity, is CHRIST CHURCH, situated near St. Margaret's Church, and the residence of W. C. Fonnereau, Esq. This building is of

CHRIST CHURCH, IPSWICH, THE RESIDENCE OF W. C. FONNEREAU, ESQ.

brick, and was erected in the very picturesque
Tudor style, about 1550, by a well-known knight,
Sir Edmund Withipol. The estate to which it
belonged passed through the noble families of
Cornwallis and Hereford, until purchased by the
ancestors of its present possessor. The interior,
particularly the hall of entrance, is well worthy a
visit, and contains some good family portraits.

CHRIST CHURCH is situated in a park, which
though of limited extent, has yet many points of
beauty, and commands by its knolls and high
grounds, an extensive view of the river Orwell,
and the country both to the right and left of that
stream. It is also well timbered, and is generally
stocked with a numerous troop of deer. The
patronage of St. Margaret's Church is in the family
of Fonnereau.

Although the house occupied by Mr. Sparrowe
may be considered as claiming the greatest architectural interest in the town, yet there are many
other habitations which either altogether, or in
part, possess features of age or curiosity, calling
upon our attention. In St. Matthew's street
stands a house formerly occupied by Sir Thomas
Hitcham, and now by W. Rodwell, Esq., of the
Elizabethan style of architecture, worthy the notice
of the antiquarian; and many private habitations
possess fragments of ancient panelling, or ornamented chimneys, attesting them to have been the
residence of wealthy individuals in the times when
perfect. In the parlour of a house of this descrip-

tion in Tacket street, for many years used as a
public house, with the appropriate cognomen of
the TANKARD, a very finely ornamented ceiling
existed, and also a handsomely carved or moulded
fire-place. The description of the latter shows to
what extent the imagination of antiquaries will
carry its possessors in endeavouring to explain that
which most probably had no meaning in the intention of the individual who had charge of its construction.

"In the Tankard public house, some curious
remains of the decorations of Sir Anthony's mansion
still exist, particularly in a large room on the ground
floor; the oak wainscot of which—beautifully
carved in festoons of flowers, and a variety of
devices—was formerly gilt, but is now painted blue
and white. The ceiling is of groined work, carved,
and wrought something after the manner of Henry
the Seventh's Chapel at Westminster. In various
compartments of this ceiling, numerous coats of
arms are sculptured, and have been emblazoned in
their proper colours; most of which are defaced,
but still several of those of the Wingfield family,
encircled with the motto of the Order of the Gar-
ter, remain in tolerable preservation. This room is
twenty-seven feet long, sixteen feet nine inches
wide, and only nine feet five inches high. The
ceiling is divided into panels sixteen inches and a
half square ; there are twelve of these in the length
of the room, and eight in the breadth : each panel
is bordered with a band, and alternately emblazoned

with a coat of arms, or filled up with a projecting ornament, in the shape of an inverted pediment, with concave sides, richly carved, and pendentive six inches from the ceiling : each of these projections terminates nearly in a point, tipped with a leaf or rose. There is one large beam intersects the ceiling, in the centre, the whole length of the room, and two smaller transverse ones—one of them a little deviating from its original horizontal position.

" Over the fire-place is a basso relievo, rudely carved in wood, and colored in a tasteless style. On our inspection of this curious relic, it was melancholy to note how the figures have been mutilated, beheaded, and defaced. We were told that this wanton mischief was principally perpetrated by the military, when this was a garrison town : and we were rejoiced to find that the sober citizens of Ipswich were not guilty of such an outrage against decency and taste.

" The interpretation of this sculpture has been thus given, agreeable to the generally received but ridiculous tradition, that it represented the battle of Bosworth Field. " Leicester town in one corner; several warriors in the centre; Sir Charles William Brandon, standard-bearer to the Earl of Richmond, lies dead by his horse, and on the other side the standard; at a distance is the earl with the crown placed upon his head by Sir William Stanley; in another is Leicester Abbey—the abbot coming out of the porch to compliment the earl." Now one would think that this was clear enough,

but the magic wand of another conjurer turns the
whole picture into the Judgment of Paris, and its
consequences, in five compartments. "In the
first," says this writer, "he appears seated, habited
in the Phrygian robe and bonnet, amusing himself
with his lute, when the three goddesses present
themselves. The next scene is his adjudgment of
the prize; when Juno, as Queen of Heaven, leads
the way, followed by Venus disclosing all her
charms, and Pallas with the Gorgon's head and
Ægis. Paris, won by the attractions of the Goddess
of Love, and her assistant son, who hovers above
in the air, decrees to her the prize which he holds
in his hand. We next view him armed *cap a pie*,
reclining perhaps at the foot of the statue of his
patroness, meditating his conquest; his lance lying
beside 'him, and his horse standing saddled and
bridled. The reclining warrior and the horse are
the only figures in the piece that could possibly
suggest the idea of the battle of Bosworth Field;
but the latter might, with as much propriety, have
been taken for the Trojan horse, as for that of
Richard the Third, or Paris for that king. Below,
in the left corner, we see Paris and some of his
friends, with horses, preparing to carry off Helen;
and, in the distance, they appear offering up their
vows in the temple of Venus, or perhaps solemnizing
their nuptials, while the horse or horses are waiting
without."

"Were we not aware into what absurdities anti-
quarians will run, when led astray by conjecture,

we should have thought it impossible that two persons could have given such different descriptions of one and the same thing; but in this, as in all other doubtful cases, we recommend our readers to see and judge for themselves. There is no appearance whatever of a warlike engagement. There is no other figure of an armed man but one; who is reclining on the ground, with a lance lying by the side of his horse, and according to the perspective, many yards in length. Now, as one soldier cannot make a battle, it clearly has no reference to the desperate conflict between Richard and Richmond. There are three female figures that cannot be mistaken, as they are portrayed in the denuded state in which the three goddesses in question are usually represented, are distinguished by their several attributes, and certainly could have no business in Bosworth Field. The principal figure, completely equipped in black armour, is reclined at the foot of what is termed in the description, "a statue to his patroness;" but which is, clearly, a pyramidical altar of considerable height, with a figure of a youthful bacchanal on the top, holding a bunch of grapes in one hand, and a goblet in the other, raised, as we may suppose, to do honour to the nuptials of Paris and Helen; which lady, from the delicacy of a bride, does not anywhere make her appearance. The artist, as was not uncommon in those days, has fallen into a palpable anachronism, by making the instrument on which Paris is amusing himself, exactly like a Spanish guitar. He is playing to three female figures, who are dancing as they approach him; and are, evidently, intended to represent the Graces, as introductory to the approach of the Goddesses, and not the three goddesses themselves, who appear in the second compartment. There is a town in the back ground, which it is difficult to determine whether it is in the clouds or on the earth, and may as well be meant for Troy as for Leicester. How the first writer could have run into such an egregious error, can only be accounted for upon the charitable supposition that he never saw the piece."

The Sir Anthony mentioned here is Sir Anthony Wingfield, a courtier of the days of Henry the Eighth, and one of the executors of that monarch. He held considerable possessions upon the spot, and the house now spoken of is believed to have been a portion of his mansion, which extended to the site now occupied by the Coach and Horses Inn in Brook Street, and indeed over the entire neighbourhood.

This relic of other times exists but in a mutilated condition. Successive inroads have been made upon its details, and it now bids fair to depart altogether. The extract we have given detailing its description is necessary, seeing the evanescent nature even of wood and stone in these days of spoliation and utilitarian alteration. Many a fair and hallowed remnant of antiquity, domestic, monumental, or ecclesiastical, torn away from its abiding place, would become forgotten, if not speedily perpetuated by description after the object itself can be no more seen. The mention of such things, when remaining in their early condition, may therefore be looked upon as an epitaph to their memory.

The streets of Ipswich, like many ancient towns, are, with few exceptions, narrow and tortuous. Modern improvements have done much to render them more convenient, though as hinted before, at the expense of some destruction. Many ancient timber houses are yet left, almost untouched by the hand of the spoiler, and let us add, long may they continue to exist in their most perfect condition. The upper, or St. Matthew's end of the town, has suffered most from this spirit, and with the exception of the house occupied by Mr. Rodwell, and to which observation has been directed, not a solitary building remains to tell a tale of its own greatness. In the lower part of the town, in the parish of St. Clement's, this is not the case. Many fine specimens of ancient domestic architecture still remain, exponents of by-gone times—the times of comfort, ease, and of wealth. We might instance in St. Clement's parish, the house occupied by Messrs. Ridley, in Fore Street—the Neptune Inn, in the same locality, and several other buildings of similar age in the Back Hamlet, and upon the road leading to Bishop's Hill. Previously to the removal of old buildings to make room for the new line of Quays, several, quaint in character, existed along the water's edge. These last, however, have given place to new and lofty warehouses, granaries, &c., while not a vestige of the original structures remain.

In a yard situate in St. Clement's, leading from the main street to the water, are the remains of an old house, which fully attest the mansion itself, in its days of perfectness, to have been of sumptuous character. On one of the corner posts of the building is carved the effigy of Queen Elizabeth, and most probably some one of her favorite courtiers—the minion of the day—equipped as Mars. Above, the little god of love appears indulging in some indecorous trick—most likely in those days not considered of questionable decency. The second floor exhibits the frame-work of a fine Tudor window, probably belonging to the principal apartment of the mansion. The builder, or ancient owner of the edifice, is not now known, his name having passed away from the records of his age. He was evidently a man living in a style of no mean character. In his days the mansion looked close upon the soft flowing Orwell—indeed its waters must have laved its very foundations. Now, buildings of no very ornamental or cleanly character, added to a line of Quays, separate it from the river, and instead of being inhabited by the man of taste and elegance, the domicile serves the purposes of a corn merchant, a basket maker, and a purveyor of coals. Various artists have executed views of this curious relic.

A house of even a more interesting character

than the one we have mentioned, stood a few years
since at the bottom of the Shire Hall Yard, at the
corner of Star Lane, and Lower Orwell Street.
The building was entirely constructed of timber,
and would seem to have been erected previously to
the use of glass for windows of domestic buildings
being known in this country. It was pulled down
a few years since, and the materials of which it was
composed sold by public auction. At the rear of
this house stood another ancient building, in
modern times used as a malt-house, but which had
evidently been consecrated to religious purposes,
possessing as it did a roof of timber, arched, and in
some degree carved. It has been supposed that
this building was the chapel of the Friars' preachers,
though not with much show of probability, as it
was smaller than would suffice for the convenience
of their community, though the locality of their
convent was close adjoining—namely, the present
Old Shire Hall Yard—upon which the building
abutted. It is not unlikely, however, that the roof
might have belonged to the genuine chapel, and at
its destruction, its timbers removed to support
the covering of a smaller edifice.

The old timber carvings still existing upon the
corner posts of houses, show that the town was
even in former times, certainly full of good habitations. Indeed there are several authorities extant
in which references are made to the fair and goodly
residences of the merchants of the place. At the
corner of Lower Brook Street and Foundation

Street, upon the side of the Half Moon public-
house, appears well carved, the old story of the
fox preaching to the geese, doubtless personifying
in all respects the condition of the town's people
with respect to their monastic superiors. Indeed
in the comparatively rude age when these carvings were made, such means were generally
used by the people, of conveying their satirical
notions of unfriendly persons to the public. It
furnishes a curious thought to us who live in days
when the printing press is the great means of praise
or blame, eulogy or satire, that the rude chisellings
upon a door post, made by a dissatisfied boor, should
survive the pompous and the stinging sarcasms of
paper and ink, though penned by the greatest
masters of satire the time furnishes.

At the corner of Cox Lane, leading out of Carr
Street, is another morsel of antiquity of similar
character to the foregoing.

At the corner of the Royal Oak public-house, in
Northgate Street, is a third carved post.

Previously to the alteration of Tavern Street, by
the construction of Bank Buildings, a curious
house, with a partial carved frontage existed. A
second house of the kind also existed at the corner
of Carr Street and Northgate Street, now occupied
by Messrs. Harmer and Ransome, wholesale drug-
gists. Its present front is completely modernized.

In St. Peter's Street, on the left hand of the
passage or thoroughfare leading to St. Nicholas'
Churchyard, stands the only remaining portion of

the house in which it is said Cardinal Wolsey was born. The remains of this building merely consist of a wall now enclosing the garden.

To speak of all the remnants of antiquity with which the town abounds, would be to perform a task, which although pleasant to ourselves, might, from its extent, tire and perplex the reader. We must be content, therefore, to dismiss the subject with a brief recommendation to those who love the study of antiquity to examine for themselves, merely saying in conclusion, that besides the numerous exterior and interior remnants remaining of domestic edifices, the works of our forefathers, several of the churches contain monuments and brasses of no common interest—objects which it is to be hoped will some day be illustrated by the artist and engraver, and be preserved for our notice and regard when those objects themselves have passed away.

EAST SUFFOLK HOSPITAL.

The East Suffolk and Ipswich Hospital is a large newly-erected structure, built on a site of ground about two acres in admeasurement, purchased for the purpose from the Rev. W. C. Fonnereau, a little to the left of the barracks, but on a much higher elevation. Every window commands a wide extent of prospect. The south side, or front, looks over the town of Ipswich, and beyond it, across the Gipping, to the hamlet of Stoke and Stoke Hills.

To the right, the view extends over Copdock, and along the Colchester road.

"The spreading Orwell, with its wood-clad sides,"

the eastern extremity of the town, and the green country beyond, are displayed on the left. The building is surrounded with a shrubbery, and the principal entrance to the house is by ascending a flight of steps, and passing through a lofty portico of the Ionic order. If pleasantness of situation, and the attainment of a pure and healthy atmosphere, enter especially into the *vade mecum* for the restoration of health, no building in the kingdom similarly set apart for the like purposes, possesses advantages exceeding this. The interior is full of convenience. On the ground floor are—the matron's store-room, the bread-room, kitchen, servants' sleeping-rooms, scullery, cellars, and other offices. On the first floor are arranged —the committee and surgeons' day rooms, the lower east ward, surgery, closets, matron's apartments, lower west ward, subscription room, and out-patient's room. On the first landing ascending the stairs, is the porter's bed-room, and apartment beyond; and on the upper floor are, the chapel and operating-room, upper east ward, east accident ward, upper west ward, west accident ward, and every convenience in closets, bath-rooms, &c., which may be necessary for the wants of the institution.

Ipswich has not boasted of the possession of an institution of this kind many years—the very name of which proclaims its objects. Mr. Richard Dykes Alexander, we believe, was the first individual who started the project, but he was soon joined by so many others, whose united services have been unremitting and effectual, that it would appear invidious to name some and not the whole.

At the period when the opening of the building took place, 3rd of August, 1836, no less than £5,000 had been raised by voluntary subscriptions among the inhabitants to found this asylum for the reception of the " halt, the blind, and the lame"— to place within the reach of the needy that surgical skill, and that medical care, which their humble circumstances would otherwise operate as a bar of deprivation. In addition to this, £300 had also been received as legacies, and the list of annual subscribers showed a revenue of £900. It was estimated that a surplus, after deducting all expenses hitherto incurred, of £2,500 would remain in hand, the interest of which, added to the subscriptions, will give an annual income of £1,000. The building itself cost £2,500, and was erected by Mr. Backhouse, of this town. A bazaar also upon the opening, held within the walls of the building, produced £300, and a sermon preached by the Rev. G. Pellew, Dean of Norwich, at St. Mary Tower, added to the funds.

We mention this latter aid to the funds for the purpose of introducing an anecdote, proving the wide-spread desire to assist in the establishment of the Hospital, as well as the eloquence of the preacher. A poor old man, whose pecuniary resources were so scanty, that he had not the means of contributing his humble mite at the church door, returned dejected to his home, regretting that "his poverty and not his will" compelled him to form, perhaps, a solitary exception to the general call on humanity. Whilst pondering on this, his forlorn condition, his eyes suddenly fell upon a pair of silver-mounted spectacles, which he had treasured up against the time when they might become of use to him. A thought struck him. He hastened to the Hospital, and laid upon one of the stalls the treasured glasses, which he requested might be received as his contribution, and in the course of a short time he had the additional satisfaction of witnessing their purchase, by Archdeacon Berners, at the price affixed—one guinea !

Among the contributors to the establishment of the institution, we must record the name of Bernard Barton, the quaker poet, who not only afforded aid by his purse, but also enlisted the assistance of his willing muse in the cause of the sick and poverty-stricken. The following beautiful address to the charitable in behalf of the object is from his pen.

"Blessed is he that considereth the Poor. The Lord will deliver him in the time of trouble. The Lord will strengthen him upon the bed of languishing; Thou wilt make all his bed in his sickness."—
Psalm xli. 1, 3.

Upon an eminence near Orwell's side,
Philanthropy her modest pile has rear'd;

Lovely the prospect, stretching far and wide,
With many a charm of sylvan beauty cheer'd :
But more by every feeling heart rever'd,
That structure built to lighten grief and pain
By gentler, purer sympathies endeared,
Than aught designed for glory or for gain,
The pyramid of pride, or Mammon's sordid fane!

Blest refuge! see the child of want and woe,
Who else had pined in sickness and despair,
Borne to thy lofty chambers, there to know
Art's healing aid, and nature's purer air.
I see him tended by as watchful care
And skill, as wait the favor'd heir of wealth;
Till science and humanity repair
Each devastation, as by magic stealth,
And send their patient forth in happiness and health !

Founded in faith, built up in hope and love,
Union its origin, and aim, and end ;
May we not hope a blessing from above
Shall on this work of charity attend,
And like the dew on Hermon's hill descend ?
Men of all *sects* and *parties* here—forgot
Their varying views—have gladly sought to blend
Harmoniously, to soothe the sufferer's lot;
Pleased, *in a world of strife*, to find one neutral spot!

Most well and wisely hath the Psalmist said,
He who considereth the poor is blest !
The Lord will strengthen him upon the bed
Of languishing;—his pillow of unrest
Shall be made smooth;—when trouble shall molest,
Deliverance shall be his from day to day ;
And deeply on his heart shall be imprest
The truth which he has made his trust and stay,
That what is giv'n the poor, God will himself repay !

The Hospital, though one of the most useful eleemosynary establishments in the town, has yet many competitors in the sphere of soothing the ills to which all flesh is heir. Numberless alms-houses have been endowed by pious and generous founders, and afford relief to indigence, straitened circumstances, and insure the rest of age—gifts of bread, and of clothing abound—and schools for both sexes, in which advancement in life as well as instruction is given, open to all classes and all ages, spread their benefits to all.

TEMPERANCE HALL.

The Temperance Hall is situated in Crown Street, at the back of St. Matthew's Street, in a situation but ill appropriated to a building of its importance or character. It was commenced in 1839, and finished in September, 1840.

In noticing a building devoted to the business and the cause of temperance, we are aware that we are performing that which few historians of towns have the opportunity of doing. We are not of those who, blind to all objections that have been made against temperance, or rather teetotalism, hold belief that such principles are those only calculated to benefit the condition of the working classes; but the fact cannot be concealed, of vast moral reformation having been produced by the means of temperance. This has been accomplished too not in isolated instances, but as regards the masses, and will continue its effects as long as the good and the philanthropic guide the course of its influence.

Greatly as the town has been benefitted by the efforts of the Society of Friends generally, and R. D. Alexander, Esq. in particular, no greater boon has been bestowed than by the erection of this noble hall—at once a proof that the charity which looks forward to perform good to those who want it, is not of that needy character which, though opening the best feelings of the heart, too often closes the strings of the purse.

THE THEATRE.

The Theatre is situated in Tacket Street, and though of a *petit* size, is yet sufficiently capacious for the town of Ipswich—at least, as regards its present inhabitants—who whether finding fault with the quality of the performances, or their tastes taking a different direction, seldom collect in large audiences within the walls. It is under the management of Mr. G. Smith, whose father has been—as indeed his son also—the manager for many years of the Norfolk circuit. During his career, several distinguished actors and actresses have trod the different boards—stars of themselves—until absorbed into the greater theatrical system of the metropolis. Here Kean has electrified his audiences with his startling action—or Young and Kemble subdued them with their tragic power. Liston, from this

stage, has made the mournful shed tears of mirth—
and a Paton or Phillips given a taste of seraphic
strains, which only belonging to creatures of

> " The gay element,
> Who play i'the plighted clouds"—

now come to us " like angel visits, few and far
between."

THE WET DOCK.

Greatly, however, as Ipswich has experienced the
progress of improvement, and the good effects of
the energy of her inhabitants, all sinks into insignifi-
cance when compared with the projection and
construction of the Wet Dock.

For many years, indeed ever since Ipswich has
been a port of any trade, the merchants and ship
owners residing in the place, and those foreigners
who visited it as traders, loudly complained that the
condition of the river, from numerous and constantly accumulating banks, and shallow waters,
checked the increase of that commerce which
under better convenience might have been attained.
There was also a cry that, in consequence of there
being no Wet Dock, as in other ports of similar
magnitude, ship owners were subjected to a serious
deterioration of their property, in addition to the
actual loss of considerable trade.   These and other
deficiencies of the port, led to the active duties of
the River Commissioners, a body which, though
not perhaps possessed of sufficient energy and

means to accomplish all that could be desired, yet
lid essential service in smoothing many of those
lifficulties in the navigation of the Orwell, which
neglected, might have become, in process of time,
insuperable. The Act under which the Commissioners were empowered was obtained in 1805,
and this body of gentlemen continued to execute
its important functions, until their duties became
absorbed, in 1837, in the more onerous undertaking
of the Wet Dock.

Many years, however, previously to the Act of
the River Commissioners being passed, Mr. Chap-
man proposed a plan of constructing a Dock somewhat similar to the present Wet Dock, proposing
to connect the basin so obtained with the open
river, at Downham Reach, by means of an artificial
channel cut along the banks of the Orwell. There
was also a second plan proposed, in order to secure
a large body of standing water near the town—
which was, that the river itself should be dammed
up at Downham Reach. Both these propositions
involving difficulties of a peculiar nature, were each
in its turn thrown by and abandoned. The
necessity, however, for forming a convenient basin
for the accommodation of the shipping frequenting
the port was day by day becoming more urgent.
Another proposal was then submitted to the inhabitants by Mr. W. Lane, the present collector of
customs, and out of this was eventually constructed,
upon the report of Mr. H. R. Palmer, civil engineer,
the plan of the Dock, in the completion of which

Ipswich has raised her character as a port to a great extent.

The primary movement in the projection of this undertaking was taken in November, 1836, when a meeting was convened of all parties, at the Town Hall, to take into consideration the formation of the Dock, and the improvement of trade. At this meeting a large assembly attended, which with small exceptions, entered fully into the eligibility of the proposed undertaking, and pledged themselves to support it. The principal reasons urged for the construction of a dock were, that—

When the magnitude of the undertaking was taken into consideration, the expense was comparatively small.—

That there was not a port between Hull and London of any magnitude equal to the Dock proposed, except at Hull, and that had two locks, which increased the expense of dues; whereas, here it was obtained at less expense.—

It would not interfere with any other interest, there not being one port between Hull and London which could command the same advantages, so that all loss by competition with others would be shut out, as none could rise in self-defence against them. The undertaking was one of great advantage, whether looked at in a private or a public view.—

The East India Trade made docks of essential advantage to every port; the expense of constructing which would be repaid by the great introduction of a traffic.—

The trade of Ipswich was rising, and would con-
inue to rise. In 1834, the duties of this Port were
:30,000., in 1836, it was £36,000., without any
nticipation of decrease. The introduction of
oreign and colonial produce would add to the gene-
al benefit of the town, by creating an increase of
rade, with a decrease of charge to the consumer.—

To prove an advantage would arise by the intro-
luction of the West India Trade, the rum sold in
:he North of Europe, was as one in eight to the
whole amount of rum imported, and this port being
one of the nearest to the Baltic, we should ultimately be able to command a great portion of that
trade.

Eventually the meeting came to the conclusion:—
To form a wet dock close to the town of Ipswich,
and to cut a new channel for the free motion of the
river water. To form embankments across the
present river, near the town, at such a distance from
each other, as to include a space of sufficient area
for a floating dock, and to cut a new channel for the
motion for the tidal water, and the discharge of the
ordinary drainage and flood water from the uplands.

The general principle of the plan was that of Mr.
Lane's, which proposed to pen up "that part of the
River Orwell which is contiguous to the town, so
that a capacious floating dock may be immediately
connected with the numerous mercantile establishments already formed upon its banks," that " a new
channel be formed, in lieu of that which is to be
enclosed, so that the tide water shall not be impeded

and that the land water shall as freely move towards the sea as it now does." The upper embankment of the dock was intended to be formed near Peter's Dock, the lower embankment about three hundred and fifty yards below the inlet which leads to the Gas Works, to embrace a sheet of water thirty-three acres, being three acres more than the London Docks, and exceeding by twenty acres the area of water in St. Catherine's Docks, in London. It was proposed to excavate the bed, giving it a depth of seventeen feet of water, from the level of the ordinary spring tide, which shall extend one hundred yards from the line of wharf, the remainder to remain until necessity requires its excavation. The entrance to be the side of the new channel, the locks to be one hundred and forty feet long, and thirty feet wide. The lower embankment, the river, and the embankments on each side of the new channel, were proposed to be forty feet in width, so as to form roadway and quays as required. No property to be injured or disturbed, with the exception of the ship-yard occupied by Messrs. Read and Page, and some alteration in Mr. Tovell's mill property, but not such as to incur any serious expense.

The estimate of expense—Earthing for the
   dock, including puddling of the bottom, and
   puddle-work in the embankment..........£16,100
Excavation of the new channel for the river.. 5,300
Deepening of the present channel.......... 5,600———
                                  £27,000

Masons', brickwork, timbers, and ironwork in
   the lock and its wing-walls, including two
   pair of gates, with the machinery for working them, mooring-posts, and rings........   6,500
Quay-wall along the face of the town, from St.
   Peter's Dock to the commencement of Mr.
   Cobbold's ooze, stone coping, oak fenders,
   steel piling, concrete, and puddling........ 14,000
Forming a quay, 30 feet wide; a sewer, 4 feet
   6 inches by 3 feet, extending from Peter's
   Dock to the outside of the town; embankments, having main holes, tide-flaps, and
   gratings ....   3,500 ——

                                  Total, 51,000
         Contingencies, 10 per cent..........   5,100
Excavating channel near Downham Reach, to avoid
   the bend in the river—say...................   2,000
                                  ————

                        Grand Total, £58,100

We have been thus particular in mentioning
this meeting, because the deviations in many essential particulars, made necessary by circumstances,
may render them at a future day of some curiosity
and interest.

As we have previously observed, the duties of
the river commissioners became absorbed in those of
the dock commission, and as a means of forwarding
the work in question it was determined that a sum
of £25,000, three per cent. consols, the accumulated
savings of the first-named body, should be transferred to the latter for the purposes of the dock act,
and that in addition, the sum of £60,000 should be
raised by loan, the commissioners giving bonds for

the repayment, with interest payable thereon at
£5. per cent., secured upon the tolls. The two
sums would make £85,000, which was considered
sufficient to complete the works. These important
matters being settled, application was made to
Parliament for an act, permissive for the construction of a dock, and regulating the amount of tolls
to be taken on vessels entering the port. After
much opposition the act was obtained, and passed
on the eighth of June, 1837. It soon afterwards
received the royal assent. H. R. Palmer, Esq.,
F. R. S., Vice President of the Institution of Civil
Engineers, was appointed engineer to the undertaking, and Mr. Thornbory became the chief contractor for the works. The first stone of the line
of quays was laid on the thirteenth of August, 1838.

On the twenty-sixth of June, 1839, the foundation of the lock was laid, amid a large concourse of
people, and attended with great rejoicings. The
stone weighed nearly four tons, and on its upper
surface appeared in a plate of bronzed iron the
following inscription.

IPSWICH DOCK.
The First Stone of this Lock was laid on the 26th day of June,
A. D., 1839,
By George Green Sampson, Esq., Mayor.
Dykes Alexander, Esq., Treasurer of the Commission.
Peter Bartholemew Long, Esq., Clerk.
Engineer—Henry R. Palmer, Esq., F. R. S. and Vice
President of the Institution of Civil Engineers.
Contractor—David Thornbory, Esq.
Nostros in Commoda Publica Conatus, tu Domine, Secunda.

The appearance of the scene was of the most imposing character. With the exception of the spot round the immediate neighbourhood of the stone, the excavation was filled with spectators, the preponderance being ladies from the town and neighbourhood. The sloping sides of the ground, as also the summit of the bank, along the whole upper side of the Lock, literally swarmed with people. Indeed, except that part of the channel where the ground was so much broken as to render standing impossible, there was not a single foot of earth unoccupied. The number of people in attendance, speaking, perhaps, within computation, and certainly not exceeding the truth, may be set down, without fear of contradiction, as 15,000. Many individuals consider there were 20,000 persons present, but this number is undoubtedly beyond the fact. All appeared animated with the highest interest towards the particular occasion that had called them together, while the beauty of the afternoon, the sun shining out with even meridian splendour—the fresh green beauty of the landscape —the Orwell covered with vessels of all sizes—the steam-packets—the gay dresses of the ladies—the military—and ever and anon the loud booming of cannon discharged from all quarters, contributed to the interest of a scene that will be remembered by those who witnessed it for many years to come.

The work proceeded with few interruptions until the month of January, 1842, when the gates of the lock being closed, the undertaking might be said to have been completed. The performance of this great work, however, cost a much larger sum than that calculated upon the original estimate ; and in 1840, the commissioners found themselves under the necessity of applying to Parliament for power to borrow £25,000 in addition to the £60,000 previously obtained. After considerable delay, trouble, and expense—and in the face of a powerful opposition raised by the General Steam Navigation Company—the requisite act was at length granted, and the preparations made to take up money on loan.

The following are the dimensions of the Dock and Lock.

Area of the Dock, 32 acres.

Length of the upper embankment, 400 feet.

Breadth of ditto, narrowest place, 25 feet.

Line of Quay, 2780 feet.

Length of lower embankment, 600 feet.

Breadth of ditto, 60 feet at top.

Depth of Lock Channel, 17 feet at high water mark.

Width of Lock Chamber, 45 feet.

Length of Channel between the upper and lower gates, 140 feet.

From the bottom of the Lock Channel to the surface of the Quay, 20 feet, 6 inches.

Whole length of inverted arch, 230 feet.

Greatest depth of foundation, 16 feet below low water mark.

Number of bricks consumed in the construction of the *Lock* only—upwards of two millions. .

Stone used in *Lock*, 600 tons.

Weight of all the materials of which the *Lock* is composed—12 thousand tons.

Possessed of a Dock of such noble dimensions, being three acres more than the whole area of the London Docks, and exceeding by twenty acres the area of water in St. Catherine's Docks, Ipswich has gathered to herself capabilities unknown to many ports of far higher pretensions. Let us hope they may be put in requisition to their full extent, and succeeding years show the cost of providing these great improvements has not been sacrificed in vain.

That Ipswich, however, has not yet availed herself of all the great means of improvement which have been fortunately—and of late years, with a boundless hand—opened to her, the non-completion of the Eastern Counties' Railway will at once testify. · Large as are the benefits to be derived from a railroad communication between this town and the metropolis, it has happened that the inhabitants have given little or no pecuniary support to the undertaking. This circumstance—and indeed not only as respects Ipswich, but also the whole county of Suffolk—has been a matter of much regret to the directors of the company, who of course have looked with confidence towards the monied interests of the locality to support the undertaking in a proportion commensurate with the importance and extent of advantages to be derived

N

from its completion. The great supporters of the
work have been merchants of Liverpool, Glasgow,
Dublin, Manchester, Birmingham, and other places.
Had the monied gentry of Suffolk but placed themselves in a position with regard to this Railway,
called for by their interest and connection with that
part of the kingdom it was intended to benefit, the
disorganizing effects of jarring interest and discord-
ant views would have been prevented, that happy
unanimity produced capable of preventing the
exhaustion and misdirection of much capital, bestowing upon us those advantages the completion
of the work would assuredly have given us many
years before the arrival of the time when we are
now appointed to see it.

The history of the origin of this national undertaking is curious, and as the "rail" itself will one
day greatly change the very relations of society, of
trade, commerce, manufactures, agriculture, connected with this town—its beginning, its growing
difficulties, and present condition, are objects as
fully a part of the history of the town itself, as the
rise of any structure in ancient time within its walls.
No apology is therefore necessary for the following
particulars connected with it.

"The act for the incorporation of this company
received the royal assent on the fourth of July, 1835.
Nearly four years elapsed before it took any considerable hold on the public mind. Early in
November, 1835, the chairman and two other
members of the provisional committee had made a

progress through Suffolk, for the purpose of personally representing to the leading gentlemen, the claims which the undertaking had to their countenance and support; and also of calling public meetings of the inhabitants to investigate and decide on its merits; and the demonstrations of local approbation which this deputation was the means of eliciting, were so numerous and decisive, as to leave the committee in no doubt that they had the hearty concurrence of the county in their endeavours to carry out the plan to a successful conclusion. But though good-will had certainly been conciliated, the confidence of the monied interests of the country, from whom alone could be expected the bulk of the large capital required for its execution, had still to be gained. In point of numbers, the shareholders residing in or connected with the county, bore a fair proportion to those having no local interest in the line, but the amount of capital subscribed for by them was little more than one-twelfth of the whole.

"Notwithstanding the success which had so far crowned exertion, the directors were still but in the midst of their difficulties. A parliamentary opposition had yet to be encountered—an opposition, as it happened, of a more than usually obstinate character. There were two rival lines in the field, both of more recent suggestion than the Eastern Counties' Railway—neither of them well suited to the wants of these counties—but both, nevertheless, very respectably supported. There was also a formidable array

of dissenting owners and occupiers, headed by gentlemen of great parliamentary influence, and to all
appearance irreconcilably opposed to the undertaking.   It was, under these circumstances, with no
ordinary anxiety that the directors proceeded before
Parliament, and by no ordinary exertions that they
were enabled to maintain their ground there, against
the serious opposition with which they were met.
So strong, however, was the case proved in evidence
for the Bill, and in so conciliatory a spirit were
the opposing parties met and arranged with out of
doors, that in a short time all opposition was at an
end, and the committee unanimously agreed to
report to the House in favour of the measure, which
concludes in the following highly recommendatory
terms :—'Your committee think it right to add, that
according to the evidence adduced, the Eastern
Counties' Railway between the termini would tra-
verse the most populous and most cultivated parts
of the counties through which it is intended to be
carried, and that great benefit would be given to
trade and agriculture by its adoption.'

"After the Bill had passed the Commons, several
new and powerful opponents sprung up, but by
meeting the parties with the same promptness and
in the same fair spirit, the Bill was finally passed by
the House of Lords, as one which was now on all
hands allowed to have for its object the accomplish-
ment of a measure of great public utility."

Time wore on, and one difficulty appearing after
another—all costly in their removal or abatement—

this line has, after seven years, not advanced towards us a third of the distance between Ipswich and London. Let us, however, trust that although "hope deferred maketh the heart sick," we may yet enjoy the good prospect which has been laid open to us, and that the ultimate realization of benefits will not altogether be denied to us.

MANUFACTURES.

Ipswich, though anciently a manufacturing town of some eminence, does not possess in modern days any particular staple of her own—if, perhaps, we except the making of ladies' stays. She possesses, however, the largest agricultural implement manufactory in England—and therefore the most extensive in the world, conducted by Messrs. Ransomes and May, the good quality and great ingenuity of whose machines are as extensively acknowledged as they are universally known. A large manufactory of Oil-cake, by Mr. Webber, Handford Mills, has also been recently established. A second Iron Foundry has also within a few years been commenced by Messrs. Bond, Turner, and Hurwood, and promises to sustain a high reputation it is fast achieving.

A large Paper Manufactory, worked by Mr. R. G. Ranson, is situated in St. Clement's. The paper at these works is almost entirely made by a single machine, and dried by hot air. The sheets can be made of any length. The machine is the invention of Mr. R. G. Ranson and his Son, and would, if generally employed, work a complete change in the manufacture, and increase the good quality of the article. The invention is protected by a patent, and has attracted the notice of the large paper manufacturers with a view to its use on license.

The principal manufactory of the port is Malt. Perhaps there is no other town of the same magnitude, in which so great a quantity of barley is manufactured into this article as at Ipswich. The stranger will soon become acquainted with this fact by noticing the many large barn-like structures, known by the name of " Maltings," and dedicated to the process which converts Sir John Barley-corn into its saccharine antetype. These structures at one period almost lined the margin of the river Orwell, though of late years many have been converted into warehouses and granaries, and the manufacture confined to the numerous alleys and bye-streets that intersect the town at almost all points.

NEWSPAPERS AND PERIODICALS.

Ipswich possesses three newspapers, two liberal, and the third tory in politics. Of these the Suffolk Chronicle (liberal) enjoys the largest circulation of any newspaper in the three counties of Suffolk, Norfolk, and Essex.

The Ipswich Journal follows the Chronicle in its amount of circulation.

The Ipswich Express (liberal) stands lowest.

The East Anglian Circular, a publication adapted to the purchaser and collector of books, is published by Mr. Burton, bookseller, Cornhill.

The Temperance Recorder, the object of which is sufficiently indicated by its title, is also issued monthly by the same publisher.

DISTINGUISHED CHARACTERS.

Having spoken of the trade, the commerce, and the historical incidents with which Ipswich has been connected, let us not forget that within its confines have flourished many men of learning, genius, and great talent. Of these we shall give a selection.

DR. WILLIAM BUTLER, M.D., born in this town, 1734, an eminent physician, and equally celebrated for wit as for physic. He died in 1816.

SIR EDWARD COKE, a name whom all lawyers must at least respect if not reverence, though not a native of Ipswich, resided frequently within it, and generally at Wherstead. Sir Edward Coke was the author of the well-known expressions of liberal sentiments, entitled "The Petition of Rights."

SIR NICHOLAS BACON, keeper of the great seal in the days of Elizabeth, deeply interested himself in the well-being of the charities of this town.

SIR CHRISTOPHER HATTON, another worthy of
Elizabeth's court, and who contrived—so the story
goes—to dance himself so far into the good graces
of his royal mistress, as to reach one of the highest
posts of the kingdom thereby, resided for a period
in a house situated near St. Mary Tower Church, in
a street named "Hatton Court" from the circumstance of its containing his residence.

NATHANIEL BACON, third son of the preceding
Nicholas, compiled the "Annals of Ipswich during
the reign of Charles the First."

THOMAS GREEN, ESQ., born in 1760, resided here
for many years, dying in 1825. Mr. Green was a
pleasant and discursive writer, his pen having been
employed on many and opposite subjects; some
of his works enjoying an extended reputation. He
published during the latter years of his life, a work,
entitled, "Extracts from the Diary of a Lover of
Literature," containing observations and criticisms
on a variety of subjects in art, science, and literature—the fruits of many years continuous study
and extended observation. In this Diary will be
found many glimpses of the characters of local
individuals, now departed to that "bourne from
whence no traveller returns," and who shed a lustre
over the circles they adorned by their learning and
talents. Mr. Green was the collector of an extensive and valuable collection of paintings by the great
masters. These adorned his residence, in Lower
Brook Street. During the life of this gentleman,
and also during the residence of his son in Ipswich

—Thomas Green, Esq.—these paintings were always open to the inspection and study of artists and amateurs, a circumstance not unattended by good results, as it was mainly through a constant reference to these masterpieces of art that Frost, an artist living in the town, corrected much of the crudity of his own genius, and enabled himself to appear before the world as a painter of undoubted power and originality of subject.

JOHN KIRBY, originally a schoolmaster and miller, published, in 1735, a topographical work, entitled "The Suffolk Traveller," the fruits of an actual survey of the county during four successive years. This book is one of the very best of its kind, and has served as a model of topographical description to the topographers of many counties. An enlarged edition was published thirty years after the death of the author, by the Rev. Richard Canning, a clergyman of much knowledge in county history, residing at Ipswich.

JOSHUA KIRBY, a well-known topographical draughtsman, resided for some years in this town. He died in 1774. He was the son of John Kirby. Several fine copies of his work were sold at the Strawberry Hill sale.

SARAH TRIMMER, the authoress of many valuable works connected with religion, and the education of youth, was the daughter of the previously-mentioned Joshua Kirby, and resided for many years in the house where the *Suffolk Chronicle* is printed.

CLARA REEVE, authoress of that well-known and pleasing fiction, "The Old English Baron"—a production which generally travels hand in hand with Walpole's "Castle of Otranto"—resided in Ipswich, her father being perpetual curate of St. Nicholas church. Clara Reeve is not only the authoress of the charming production we have named, but many others, the fame of which has not survived so strongly.

Although Ipswich cannot claim the honour of the birth of THOMAS GAINSBOROUGH, the great painter of English landscapes, yet it was in this town his great genius became apparent, and won for him a patron who greatly assisted in bringing him before the public.

PRISCILLA WAKEFIELD, a well-known instructress of youth through the instrumentality of her pen, resided in this town many years.

BERNARD BARTON, the poet, though not born here, received his education in this town, and resides at Woodbridge. To speak of the productions of Bernard Barton is unnecessary in this volume. Many are the hearts exalted in their aspirations by the muse of the Quaker poet. He still lives in his calm retreat at Woodbridge, like one

> " Secluded but not buried,
>   And with song cheering his days."

Endeared to an extensive circle of friends by the sociality of his disposition, the kindliness and simplicity of his nature, as well as the brightness of his intellect and the purity of his life, he exists an example that goodness adds lustre to genius; and though the mere possession of talents induces the world to gaze and admire, it is only when accompanied by virtues that we can satisfactorily rest upon them, and love the possessor.

It may here be appropriate to mention Miss Lucy Barton, the daughter of the poet, who though not possessing her father's poetical talents, has pleasingly and extensively distinguished herself by the publication of several books for young people, both in verse and prose.

Nor ought we to omit to mention another lady, a native of this place, who promises to become an ornament and acquisition to our English literature. As her retiring disposition induces her on all occasions to conceal her name, we will only say that those who have read "*Historic Reveries*" will not think that our anticipations are too great.

The Rev. JAMES FORD, late incumbent of St. Lawrence church in this town, is the author of several works in religion and biography. This gentleman is an antiquarian of considerable knowledge and research.

GEORGE FROST, a Suffolk artist of note, resided in this town many years, and died here in 1821. The paintings and drawings of Frost are known and prized far beyond the county of Suffolk. They consist mostly of views in the locality, and are distinguished generally by a strict adhesion to the appearance of nature, without any of the gaudy

colouring and glittering lights of paintings of the
modern school. Several views of ancient places in
Ipswich, painted by Frost, have been engraved.
It was the opinion of the late Mr. Green, an
enlightened judge, that had not Frost so deeply
imbued himself with the spirit of his favourite master, Gainsborough, both in style of composition
and colouring—his original genius would have
more especially distinguished itself. It is said
that Frost himself in his latter days became of the
same opinion, and that he has been heard to
exclaim, "I have been spoilt by Gainsborough."

It is singular that a county possessing so
few fine views or prospects, should yet have
produced the two greatest masters in English
landscape which the English school possesses.
Within the confines of Suffolk, however, the great
geniuses of Gainsborough and Constable were
ripened, and many of the best portions of their
most renowned compositions have been but tran-
scripts of their early sketches transferred to the
canvass of maturer years. A third painter of cele-
brity, Old Crome, though more closely connected
with the sister county of Norfolk, is also indebted
to Suffolk for the subjects of many of his best productions. The same might perhaps be said of his
son, a living artist. A fifth name in art is also
much indebted to this county—the present Mr.
Starke. We are bound also to mention a sixth as
taking his inspiration from the pastoral, heathy,
and woody scenes of Suffolk, Thomas Churchyard,

of Woodbridge, who, though an amateur, evinces the power, originality, and facility of hand possessed by few masters.

Although neither distinguished in art or literature, the name of HENRY TOOLEY (or Tolye) must not be left unmentioned among our worthies. A munificent benefactor to the town and port of Ipswich, and providing as he did during his lifetime, and by his will, funds amply sufficient to found several alms-houses and support their inmates, he is surely entitled to notice and regard. Henry Tooley was a portman of Ipswich, and died about the year 1550. The revenue arising from Tooley's charity estates exceed £1000 per annum.

THOMAS CLARKSON, ESQ., one of the great pioneers towards the abolition of slavery, though not a native of Suffolk, has for many years resided at Playford Hall, a few miles from the town. No reference is needed by us to the noble deeds of Thomas Clarkson. He stands a bright luminary among the philanthropists of the earth, upon which all men gaze.

We have now given in the foregoing pages, a synopsis of the ancient and modern condition of Ipswich—with notices of its public buildings—its trade and commercial position. The task completed, let us in conclusion hope that as she increases in importance, extent, and population, some more worthy offering may be made towards her history than the imperfect memorials yet extant of

her.   Independently of the details of her rise in the
scale of uimportant places through the murky and
unsettled atmosphere of ages now gone by, exists many
a curious legend for the lover of the romantic, and
numerous characters yet unchronicled by the studious biographer.   Well will her early annals repay
perusal, and prove how truly wrote the poet, when
he penned the well-known lines.

> " Nor rude nor barren are the winding ways
>   Of hoar antiquity, but strewn with flowers."

OBJECTS OF INTEREST IN THE COUNTY AND TO
WHICH THE TOURIST CAN EASILY GAIN ACCESS.

Bury St. Edmund's contains fine remains of a
renowned abbey, and other monastical antiquities.

Lavenham possesses one of the finest gothic
churches in the county.   The details of this building have been repeatedly engraved for the use of
architects.

Hadleigh possesses a fine church.   This town
was the residence of Dr. Drake, the well-known
Shakesperian commentator.   Dr. Taylor, a martyr
to the tenets of protestantism was burnt alive on a
common near Hadleigh.   A stone, with an ancient
inscription, marks the spot.

At Melford is a magnificent church of gothic
architecture, containing many good monuments.

At Clare are the remnants of a feudal castle, the ossessions of Richard Fitz-Gilbert—father of the elebrated Richard Strongbow.

At Freston is a lofty ancient tower, commanding n extensive view of the Orwell.

At Woolpit is a church of fine florid gothic. The porch is particularly worthy of notice.

At Thetford, a portion of which town is in ¡uffolk, are the remains of monastical and feudal ¡uildings.

At Leiston are the remains of a fine abbey.

At Bungay are the remnants of a castle, an ancient ¡eat of the Bigods.

At Butley stand the fine remains of an abbey.

At Wingfield is a fine church, containing the monuments of the De la Pole family, including that of De la Pole, Duke of Suffolk, the supposed murderer of the "good Duke Humphrey." Here is also a portion of his stronghold, Wingfield castle, now converted into a modern residence.

Dunwich, called the " Ruined City," lies on the east coast. The greater part of the town has been swallowed by the sea. Many churches and monasteries have been at various periods overwhelmed.

At Framlingham are the remains of a castle, the seat of the Bigods, Mowbrays, and Howards. In the church are several fine monuments of the Norfolk family, and that of Surrey, the poet.

At Languard is a fortress well worthy the attention of the tourist.

The visitor is also recommended on no account

to omit a steam boat trip upon the Orwell from Ipswich to Harwich, in which his eye will be gratified with a succession of noble and interesting views unsurpassed by the rivers of any other part of the kingdom.

For a full account of places and objects of interest in the county, the stranger is referred to Wodderspoon's " Historic Sites of Suffolk." Many of the most interesting remains are also engraved in Davey's Suffolk Antiquities.

BURTON, PRINTER, IPSWICH.